The Gift
of a
Broken Heart

AVERY GARRETT LONG

The Gift of a Broken Heart is a work of nonfiction.

Some names and identifying details have been changed.

Cover Design by Avery Garrett Long

Published in the United States by *With All My Heart 323 Publishing*

WithAllMyHeart323@gmail.com

ISBN: 9781719825320

DEDICATION

This book is dedicated to the Hero of this Story,

and to all those who broke my heart along the way,

leading me into His Loving Arms.

.

AVERY GARRETT LONG

TABLE OF CONTENTS

AVERY GARRETT LONG

Introduction

This is not your typical love story, but it is a love story. There is a Knight in Shining Armor. There is a Damsel in Distress. There is also pursuing, wooing, battling, rescuing, and great courage. There is definitely True Love.

This is the story of a rare Knight, who, through years of perseverance and with infinite patience, finally managed to win the heart of this frightened little damsel. Understanding that her heart had been broken by so many others, He took the time to earn her trust, never pushing, never rushing, but never giving up. He remained faithful, even when she could not. Seeing past her many weaknesses to the beauty underneath, He relentlessly pursued no matter how much she ran. Over time, He was able to teach her the meaning of true love by His example until she finally, finally was able to let go and rest in that love, set free at long last to be her true self. To love and be loved. And in being loved, truly loved, she found the strength to see the beauty in her suffering and the courage to follow her heart and live her dreams.

That damsel, of course, is me. I have loved others and been loved. Still there is only One love of my life. One who has taught me the meaning of love, which is simply this...

> *"Love is patient and kind, it does not get jealous or brag.*
> *It is not proud, it does not force itself on others.*
> *It is not selfish, it is not easily angered,*
> *it keeps no record of wrongs.*
> *It does not delight in evil, but rejoices with the truth.*
> *It always protects, always trusts, always hopes,*
> *always perseveres. LOVE NEVER FAILS."*
> - I Corinthians 13:4-8

There is only One who has been able to love me that faithfully and unconditionally. This story is about that One.

PART
ONE

AVERY GARRETT LONG

Prologue

The Call

It all started when I was 15 years old. Well, it probably started long before that, but this is when I consciously checked into the story. I was raised in a traditional church, though it did not seem to have much to do with our family's everyday life. It was just something we did on Sundays. During my early years, I really did not give God or faith much thought. I went to church because my mother told me to. When I was 12, I went through the "Confirmation" classes and officially became a member of our church because that is what we did. None of it meant anything to me.

I began to experiment with drugs and alcohol as a young teenager without any conviction. I was not too openly rebellious. I did my church thing as required and then went out to party with my friends. Until one day, something (or should I say Someone) began to tug at my heart.

I met some young followers of Christ who were genuinely excited about their faith and it got my attention. I had always observed a sincere and deep felt faith in both of my maternal grandparents, but that seemed only for old people who did not need to have fun. I had an impression of God as a harsh disciplinarian who frowned upon the idea of enjoying life; everything you like to do is bad and all the things you were supposed to do were boring. These young believers, however, seemed to be having lots of fun, so I began to reconsider my beliefs.

I struggled for some time between this desire for a deeper meaning to life and my idea that if I decided to follow God, He would immediately give me a list of do's and don'ts; most of all, **don't** have any fun. Then one evening, after a service in which I felt a powerful loving Presence calling to my heart, I found myself walking up to that altar to answer it. I knelt at the altar of my grandparent's church and was overwhelmed with the strongest sense of love that I had ever felt. This is what I prayed:

"Lord, I want to go all the way with You. I want everything You have for me."

I have no idea why those words came out of my mouth. This was not an idea that I had ever heard from anyone else. All I know is that I meant it - with all my heart. And I believe that prayer forever changed my life. I meant it then, and, in spite of all that I have been through, I still have not changed my mind. Perhaps if I had known what it would cost me, I might have thought twice about it, but I am glad I did not.

Today, 40 years later, I am grateful that God took me seriously and I cannot regret the journey it has led me on. Yes, it has cost me much, but the blessings have been so much greater.

I cannot tell you that my life dramatically changed after that prayer. It still took me several years to stop running. After that, I spent many years trying to perfect myself. Yet ever so slowly, Grace began to sink in and transform me. I floundered through a long dark tunnel for years and then I began to learn the lessons that only deep suffering can teach.

For over 20 years, my life looked like any other typical middle class young woman trying to raise a family, keep a marriage together and be true to my faith. Then my life took a sudden sharp and terrifying turn that no one saw coming, least of all me. I thought that trusting in God was difficult when my life was normal, but my life will never be normal again. The challenges and heartaches I faced through this turn of events tested my faith to the breaking point but

God endured. Looking back, I can see how God was preparing me for this extremely traumatic time in my life, teaching me lessons that I would desperately need. You never know what you can survive until you have to survive it, but I know that I am literally alive today because I had discovered this Love that could carry me through even the most devastating storms.

The pages you are about to read are merely entries from my journals over the years. Most of them were only meant to be shared with those closest to me; some of them I never intended to share with anyone. I believe, however, that God has asked me to take this vulnerable step of humbly laying these parts of my life bare before you. If you find this book in your hands, I have prayed for **you** and I believe our meeting is by Divine destination. My hopeful prayer for you is that, through my inadequate words, I can manage convey what I have learned about the most Amazing, Beautiful Love that has ever existed. This Infinite Love that has called to me and that calls to each of us. If my story could convince you of just one thing, it would be this...You are worthy of love and YOU ARE LOVED. No strings attached.

Chapter 1

The Awakening

April 1, Confirmation

*"We know that no one is made right
with God by obeying the law.
It is by believing in Jesus Christ."*
- Galatians 2:16

I was cleaning out my nightstand the other day, and I came across a number of articles and books with sections that I had highlighted as well as some of my old journals. While reading them, I was surprised to see many of the same ideas that have just lately been an integral part of recent revelations in my spiritual journey. I thought, *"I've been here before. Why did it not stick then? What was missing that caused me to continue wandering around in the dark for these past 8 years? What was I thinking then?"* Since I did not have enough journaling from those times to know what I was thinking, I do not have the answers to those questions. That frustration motivated me to start writing down my story - for myself, to encourage me in the times of doubting and darkness, and for those that love me, so they can share my experience with me. So that is how this blog began. That is when I began to see the light at the end of my long, dark tunnel.

I have been reading a book recently in which the author encourages Christians to depend on Christ rather than on their works and the approval of one another. That message resonated with me. I have found that this performance type of thinking tends to feed my perfectionist tendencies, which encourages me to try to earn God's approval. Having battled with this mentality for years, I have certainly learned that working to get approval from God or humans does not result in the fulfilling life that I crave. So I understand that this does not work, but I have no idea how to achieve what I do want in my life. On the other hand, if it is not mine to achieve, will God ever accomplish it? Is this hope of intimacy with God just a pipedream? Could I ever experience the peace and joy that so many Christians speak of but so few actually seem to have? Will I just wander around in the "desert" for the rest of my life searching for this silent, evasive God - searching for meaning? I was left with more questions than answers, but that was just the beginning.

April 2, Captivating

I read another book that a friend gave to me about the longing in a woman's heart to be loved. I cried through the whole book. As little girls, we have this need for validation, and naturally, many of us first look for it from our fathers. We want to know if we are special, beautiful, lovable. For many of us, the answer we get is *"No, you are not that beautiful or special. You are not quite good enough. You are not worth the effort."* We then spend the rest of our lives trying to find that validation somewhere else; trying to find a *"yes"* to our questions. The message that we often get as women from the men in our lives is that we are not enough, or maybe, even worse, that we are too much.

I believe that God placed this longing in our hearts to be cherished, romanced, worthy of pursuing and fighting for. Yet those desires and the reality of our lives are often far apart, resulting in a sense of inadequacy, shame and frustration. If only we were *"enough"* or not *"too much"*, we could be loved the way we long to be. So we spend our lives laboring to be whatever it is that makes us lovable and worthy to others, instead of being free to be the women God created us to be. Deep down, we fear there is something terribly wrong with us; we can never measure up. Many of us just plain give up and close down our hearts when the wounds become too many. It is safer to guard our hearts, to hide and shut everyone out. Maybe if they see who I really am, they will find me to be a great disappointment.

As I recognized my own life in this description, I began to hear God calling to me, *"I've been listening to your heart, Avery. I know your pain, your longings. You are not going crazy; you are not weird. You are just exactly how I made you. You are not alone. I am here. I understand your heart and I love it. You are beautiful; you are worth pursuing; you are worth fighting for...to Me."*

This past week of tears have left my eyes swollen and red, but they were good tears, healing tears. I could feel the very deepest wounds in my heart beginning to heal. Could it be true that God really loves me? That I am beautiful to God? I think, maybe, for the first time in my life, I am beginning to believe that.

April 3, The Need

"Because you belong to Christ,
you have everything you need."
- Colossians 2:10

I began to realize that I have looked to everyone and everything but God to meet the needs of my heart, even while considering myself one of His followers. I have often been convinced that I could be happy if only my husband would love me the way he "should". Even though the love of a partner can be affirming and healing, our validation needs to come from within first. It may be natural to bring this need to our loved ones, but in the end, it will only leave us feeling empty and frustrated, and can even be damaging to our relationships. I recognized that, no matter how hard he may try, my husband cannot fill me, and the more I push, the more I will push him away. It became clear to me that to have real love with my husband (or anyone else), I must let go of expectations and stop bringing this longing to him.

Therefore, if only God can meet this hunger in my heart, then I made a decision that I would take all my needs to God and see what happens. This was a challenge for me, since trusting God has never been my strong suit. Nonetheless, that is what I began to do - bring every little need to God. I stopped looking to my husband or to anyone or anything else but God to fill me. With the pressure off, I am finding myself more able to accept what others have to give to me. That is when my tormented heart began to find peace.

April 5, My Filthy Rags

> *"...All our righteous acts are like filthy rags."*
> - Isaiah 64:6

As I have already admitted, I am a perfectionist. I have a perfectionist father so I come by it honestly. My natural tendency is to try to do everything perfect. I wanted to be the perfect Christian, perfect wife, perfect mother, perfect whatever.

Several years ago, God began teaching me about grace and setting me free from all the rules I had set up for myself. I started to truly understand that a life of faith is not lived by following the rules, but by following the Spirit. I suppose the truth is that you may not even be able to tell the difference by looking from the outside of a person. Yet the difference on the inside is phenomenal.

Jesus spoke about the blindness of the "white-washed" Pharisees, claiming that the tax collectors and sinners were often more likely to repent because their sin was easy for all to recognize. The Pharisees were respected in society because they looked good on the outside, while the sinners were judged and rejected because they looked bad on the outside. Yet, to God all sin is the same and "***all have sinned and fall short of the glory of God***" (Romans 3:23).

It seems to me that the "sinners" had a great advantage; they could easily see their need for God's grace and mercy. This tends to humble you. Like the Pharisees, my perfectionist personality created a sense of pride and independence that actually, rather than being pleasing to God, as I believed, was a stumbling block.

I learned to enjoy the freedom in Christ that I was experiencing.

"Whom the Son has set free will be free indeed" (John 8:36).

Eventually, however, this freedom was not totally satisfying because, while I was able to understand what a Christian is not, I still could not quite grasp what a Christian really is. Furthermore, I still was not finding that intimacy with God for which I have longed since I was 15 years old.

It is strange how you can understand something with your mind for years, and then one day God manages to get it into your heart and it comes alive. Lately, God seems to be getting through to me about things I thought I understood, and the result is that I feel like a blind woman who has been given sight.

Long ago, I understood how simple a relationship with God is, before I complicated it. My good works are filthy rags. I do not need to strive to win God's approval. I do not need to worry about tomorrow. I do not need to achieve my own holiness (and I could not if I tried; which I did). I do not need to attain intimacy with Christ. I simply need to trust God like a little child and take one day at a time.

April 6, God's Voice

"Then He said, 'Go out and stand on the mountain in the Lord's presence.' At that moment, the Lord passed by. A great and mighty wind was tearing at the mountains and was shattering cliffs before the Lord, but the Lord was not in the wind. After the wind, there was an earthquake, but the Lord was not in the earthquake. After the earthquake, there was a fire, but the Lord was not in the fire. And after the fire there was a voice, a soft whisper."
- 1 Kings 19:11-12

I have always wanted to hear God's voice. At times, I have felt sure that I have. More often, I have pleaded with God to speak to me and felt like my prayers never went beyond the ceiling. I am not saying I expected a booming voice from the sky or that I needed a burning bush or anything. Just some kind of clear reassurance of God's presence; whatever that means. Basically, I just did not want to doubt anymore that He is there and that He cares. But I did.

As God has begun opening my eyes lately, I have had this most incredible recognition. Like everything else He has been showing me, it is so obvious and simple. I find myself feeling a bit slow for not catching on sooner but grateful that God finally got it from my head to my heart.

I can see now that God speaks to me all the time, but I have not been confident in that Voice. His way is not loud and dramatic; His voice is quiet and gentle. As I Kings 19 says, the Lord is not in the wind, the earthquake or the fire, but in the gentle whisper - the small still voice. We have this tendency to expect our relationship with God always to be dramatic and exciting, or else He must be ignoring us. Sometimes we will have those mountaintop moments with God, but more often we will be learning to walk by faith, not by sight. The temptation is to want to keep those mountaintop experiences going and keep our emotions stirred up, always looking for the next high. This is so dangerous as it causes us to be misled into trying to duplicate them and frequently left feeling dissatisfied with our lives. Maybe that is why there is such a drug epidemic these days. We have gotten the idea that life is supposed to feel good all the time and something is wrong if it does not.

I recently read an illustration that was helpful to me. When my child is doing my will, she will hear nothing from me. If, for instance, I have told her not to ride her bike on the street and I look out the window to see that she is riding her bike on the sidewalk, I am content to enjoy watching her out there having fun. However, if I were to look out the window and see that she is riding in the street, I am going to get out there and call for her to get off the street. So maybe it is the same with God. If I am in His will, I hear nothing. God is simply enjoying me.

I do not think being in God's will is too complicated. I choose to be in God's will, I pray for God's will and then just believe that it will be. If I do wander off the "sidewalk", I can trust that God will let me know, just as I would let my beloved child know.

I think I have always had it backwards. I wanted God to shout to me or give me miraculous signs to tell me His will. *"AVERY, STAY ON THE SIDEWALK. DON'T FORGET TO STAY ON THE SIDEWALK. LET ME EXPLAIN TO YOU HOW TO STAY ON THE SIDEWALK!"* Meanwhile, I have been on the sidewalk the whole time. Now that I think about it, that actually is the way I have been parented my whole life, and it is kind of insulting. I guess it makes sense that I would expect this and believe something is wrong without it, but I prefer the vote of confidence of a Father who counts on my ability and willingness to do what He has asked of me.

It comes back to trust again, doesn't it? If I trust God, then I believe He is capable of keeping me in His will and guiding me. I love that! I have made it so hard for so long, telling myself that God did not care, was not interested in me. Now I can see that I just wanted God to fit into my mold instead of accepting His way. That bit of awareness has changed how I feel about God's love. I do not know exactly how to explain it, but I just know He is there now and I do not feel the need to jump up and down to try to get His attention. He is there; He is listening; and I do know His voice after all.

April 7, My Feelings

Although I concede that God is love, my feelings sometimes tell me otherwise. My feelings have convinced me at times that God is not there for me, that God will not hear me, that He will judge me and I will be found unacceptable, and that He may even kill someone I love to get my attention.

As I have said, we tend to view God from the perspective of our relationship with our earthly father, so my feelings about God should not be surprising. This is why it has been so hard for me to trust God. Yet my emotions sometimes deceive me, because God is not like my earthly father. Since, for years, I have been in a conflict between what I believe and what I feel about God, I have found it much easier to run to my idols for comfort than to my God. Even though I know that my father loved me and did his best, sometimes when I was young and ran to him, I did not get the loving response that I needed. As a result, my gut reaction has not been to run to God. He might let me down as well.

Some idols are obviously harmful, like drugs; others seem harmless or acceptable like food, shopping, TV. The most dangerous to me are the ones that are respected and admired; the ones that we can use to make us feel worthy and valuable, which can even include Christian ministry. I have been guilty of using that to feel better about myself. God showed me that some of the most innocent things I was doing had become my idols. Isn't reading a good thing? Yet I ran to my books for comfort when I was hurting rather than running to God. Anything can be an idol. It is a matter of where my heart is.

Fortunately, because God wants me to run to Him, He would not let my idols satisfy me. He wanted me to conclude that only He can fulfill me. He alone is worthy of my complete devotion. So I gave God my idols and He took them. It does not mean I will not ever be tempted to try to take them back. Still I can see now that I do not need them anymore.

I do not have to be confused by my emotions anymore. All I have to do is open the door to my heart and let God in. I can count on God because His love is not weak and flawed like human love - because God **is** love.

April 8, Dealing with My Enemy

> *"Put on all of God's armor so that you will be able to stand firm against all strategies of the devil.*

For we are not fighting against flesh-and-blood enemies,
but against evil rulers and authorities of the unseen world,
against mighty powers in this dark world,
and against evil spirits in the heavenly places."
- Ephesians 6:11-12

As much as God loves me, Satan hates me. Through all these years of darkness, my enemy has bombarded me with messages such as *"God has abandoned you. He is not here; He does not love you. He does not even like you. Why would He? No one does. God is probably not even real anyway. You have just been brainwashed. You cannot do anything right. You are a failure at everything you do. No one appreciates you. Your family would be better off without you. The world would be a better place if you just die!"* I am sorry to say that, at times, I bought all of it. Yet I never recognized it for what it was - an attack on my spirit. I did not understand that God was right there beside me in my darkness, strengthening my faith.

It's scary in the darkness. It can make you desperate, bringing out the worst in you - at least, it did in me. In my desperation, my self-centered nature became very evident. I did not understand that I was dealing not only with the deceit of my own insecurities, but with the lying enemy of my soul as well. As God began to bring me back into the light, I realized that two spirits in particular - depression and self-pity - have plagued me. I felt a little silly but I began to rebuke those spirits. I kept doing it every day, until one day, I noticed that they were completely gone. Not only that, but I actually felt joyful; it took me awhile to recognize that feeling. But yes, I do remember joy!

So now, when I feel any of these old negative emotions creeping back, I pray, but I also use my authority in Christ. I see now that so many of my negative emotions are spiritual attacks. However, I have weapons - I do not have to be a helpless victim. I dusted off my weapons and I intend to use them regularly now. I have lately made a conscious effort to put on the Armor of God each morning. It may sound hokey, but this is war and it has lately become very real to me.

Trying to fight it on my own, I was constantly defeated, but in Christ, I am always the winner.

Chapter 2

Abounding in Love

April 12, God Loves Me

I had a beautiful reminder today of God's love. It was actually
something that happened to my daughter, not me, but God used it to
show His love to both of us. As it just so happened, this morning, I
had been speaking honestly to God about my doubts about Him.
After years of witnessing so much that is empty, phony and just plain
wrong done in the name of Christ, I can at times be somewhat
cynical about religion. I have probably even rejected some of the
good along with the bad. In fact, at times I have even been unsure
about my belief in the God of the Bible at all - being tempted to
"throw the baby out with the bathwater", as they say.

I have wrestled with my faith for many years, and while I have
made my peace with it for the most part, there are still days I
question and doubt. Today was one of them. I shared my thoughts
with God; I did not challenge Him to prove Himself to me (as I have
probably done so many times in the past); I just asked God to forgive
my doubts and help my unbelief. I believe He answered that prayer
through my daughter, as I later talked with her on the phone. She was
in a bad mood, because she was planning to quit her job that day. She
had been in an unhappy relationship for the past year and felt she
really needed to come home for the summer to get away and heal.
Unfortunately, she was hired for this job on the condition that she
stay through the summer and not only did she not want to let them

down, but she also wanted to be able to return to work there in the fall when she went back for school.

The supervisor came to speak to her before she had the chance to bring up the issue. To my daughter's complete surprise, her employer asked if she wanted to go home for the summer and come back in the fall, because there was another girl who was looking for a summer job. Once realizing that they were on the same page, her supervisor exclaimed that God must have worked it out for her. My daughter called me right away and said, "*God loves me!*"

I said, "*I know*". She then told me the story that left us both feeling very special to our Heavenly Father. As I hung up the phone, I sighed contentedly, "Yes, *God loves me, too. Didn't I already know that?*"

April 16, Regret and Gratitude

"I am not in the least ashamed.
For I know the One in whom I have placed my confidence,
and I am perfectly certain that the work He has committed
to me is safe in His hands until that day."
- 2 Timothy 1:12

Today is a blue Monday for me. I woke up feeling that familiar *"I want to stay in bed and hide from the world"* feeling this morning. So I gave it to the Lord and prayed for comfort. Then I drug myself up to start my day.

I recently met a fellow homeschooling mother with nine children. She amazes me. She really seems to have her "act together" and her kids seem so perfect. Wonder woman! While being around a woman like that is somewhat intimidating, she is straightforward and down-to-earth, and I actually like her. She seems to have what I have spent my life trying to achieve - the successful homeschooling family.

I understand that looking good to others is not what is important. Maybe that is meaningless to God and only serves to feed our pride, making it harder to admit our need for Him. Nonetheless, my vanity and my desire for my children's happiness make it a hard

20

pill for me to swallow that I have been unable to create that idyllic family environment for which I have strived so long. I thought that maybe I should have been stronger and hung in there with homeschooling my kids for longer. Maybe they would not have had so many problems and heartaches. On the other hand, maybe they would have been better off if I had never homeschooled them at all. To be quite honest, women like my Wonder Woman friend make me feel like a total flop as a mother. I went to bed convincing myself that my kids are in a better place to see their need for God's grace and that is what is important for me.

This morning, however, I could see that my depressed feelings had their root in my sense of failure. Within a few minutes, I was able to get to the heart of the matter. When my mother died almost 8 years ago, I plummeted into a depression. During that time, I somewhat checked out on my family for a while. I spent several years so consumed with self-pity, my grief, my discouragement, my sense of failure, my pride, my loneliness, myself - ME, ME, ME - that I have let my family down. I cried bitterly for all the lost time that my family needed me and I have not been there for them. I grieved for how my selfishness has hurt the ones I love the most. All those wasted years and the damage it has done to my children and my marriage. I asked God to forgive me. I asked my husband and my children to forgive me. Every time I think that God could not possibly humble me more, He shows me yet a deeper glimpse into the wretchedness of my own soul.

I would like to say now that I have seen the light and will "turn over a new leaf". I will put aside my selfishness and be the beautiful woman of God that I so want to be. Yet I know better now. I spent many years trying to do just that - to be the perfect Christian woman. Then I spent more years feeling sorry for myself because I could not and blaming others for my feelings of defeat. Now I understand that any goodness in me can only be accomplished by God, so all I can do is surrender to Him. All these years of my effort have brought me back to square one - what I have known all along. **He** is able to accomplish that which I have committed to Him. My work is simply to give it all to God and try to stay out of the way. Actually, that is hard enough!

April 17, School Tragedy

I will never forget yesterday for as long as I live. Little did I know when I woke up to my blue Monday that my daughter was facing the greatest terror of her life. I was just minding my own business, oblivious to the world outside my home, when the phone rang. It was my daughter Calah. *"I just wanted you to know that I'm alive, Mom."*

"I'm happy to hear that, Calah. Was there some reason that I should be concerned that you weren't?" That is how one of the most horrific days in the history of our country began for me. Calah went on to explain to me that she was walking across her college campus to class when she heard gunshots. She wisely turned around and went back to her dorm where she remained for the entire day. That decision probably literally saved her life. She explained to me on the phone that someone had been killed that morning and the school authorities were telling students to stay locked in their dorms and stay away from windows. Still, she had no idea of the magnitude of chaos that was all around her. She and I kept in close touch all day. She became very frightened when she saw at least 100 police officers, guns ready, outside her dorm window. Soon there were SWAT teams wandering through her building, warning the students to stay locked inside. The news began to come out that not just one, but many people had been shot. There were rumors of a gunman lining students up and shooting them execution style. Some said there were several gunmen. Rumors of bombs. I wanted to take comfort in the fact that my daughter was safely locked in her dorm, but with so little information and so many rumors, I was not comforted; I was terrified and frustrated. I wanted to race down there and save my daughter. I

knew, however, that I could get nowhere near that campus and I certainly did not want her wandering around outside to come to me. There was not a thing I could do but pray.

As the number of confirmed casualties grew, my heart sank. I could easily imagine being one of those parents whose lives were instantly shattered and I grieved for them. I very nearly *was* one of them. It was a long, scary day, and I spent it glued to the news, praying and answering the phone calls of concerned friends and relatives. I was grateful for all the love and support, as I spoke with people from all around the country - some that I had not spoken to in years.

As evening arrived, it was unclear if there were still any shooters wandering around the campus. Calah insisted it was too dangerous and there was no reason for us to come. Yes, I thought. There is a reason. I need to hold my baby, look at her sweet face and reassure myself. We were exhausted, however, and did not know if we would even be able to get anywhere near the campus, so we respected her wishes to wait. I went to bed early with a splitting headache and had a terrible, restless night's sleep.

This morning, I spoke with Calah as soon as she was awake. She said she also had a bad night. She was thinking about how she would feel if her boyfriend had been one of the victims and then she understood how we felt. She knew why I wanted to come and hug her. They are closing the school for the rest of the week, so I am going to go get my little girl and give her the biggest hug I can and maybe never let go. Mother-love is a powerful thing.

April 18, What Evil Meant for Our Harm

Calah is home now. All I want to do is look at her beautiful face, listen to her sweet, gentle voice and hug her constantly. Even as my heart goes out to the grieving families, I am also filled with gratitude.

We call this a senseless tragedy. It is certainly tragic and there is certainly no sense in the killing of these innocent people, many just at the beginning of their lives. Yet, is it true that God can bring good from even such horrendous acts of evil? For those who are experiencing a personal loss, it might take a long time to believe that anything good could come from this horror. I can sure understand that and I in no way want to minimize their pain.

For me, however, God has used this terrible scare to remind me of what really matters. Too often, with my negative thinking tendencies, I have centered more on what is wrong with my life rather than what is right. When death brushes closely by, you remember that the people you love are gifts to treasure every day. None of us has any guarantee of tomorrow. I was reminded not only to be thankful for Calah's safety, but for all the special people in my life who love me and for all that God has given to me. Something can always be found about which to complain or instead there is always plenty for which we can rejoice. I have a choice. I choose to be grateful.

In addition to gratitude, it is important to let your loved ones know how much they mean to you. When bad things happen, we vow to be more faithful to express our love. As the memories fade, there is a tendency to forget our promise and take people for granted again. Human nature, I suppose.

I come from an affectionate family. My mom and I often expressed our love for one another. When she died, though, I would have given anything in the world to be able to tell her one more time how much I love her. I still feel that way eight years later. Maybe one day I will be able to tell her again, but on this earth, I no longer have that privilege. However, for the rest of my loved ones, I can keep saying it and it can never be too often.

Another beautiful thing that comes from tragedies like this is the way people come together to support one another. We forget all our petty bickering, our religious, political and cultural differences, and remember what matters - we are all brothers and sisters and when one of us hurts, we all hurt.

Today, I took Calah out for lunch. As our hostess seated us, she noticed Calah's college sweatshirt and said, *"Can I just give you a hug?"* She then turned to me and said, *"Let me give you one, too."* Calah and I welcomed her warm, sincere hug, and thanked her, both so choked up that we struggled to maintain our composure. Later, the hostess returned to our table with some chocolate cake, *"on the house"*. As she served it to us, she explained, "*My grandmother always said, 'Chocolate doesn't fix everything, but it sure does help.'*" Amen to that. And it did. Although, more than the cake, this stranger's compassion was a healing balm for us.

That is exactly the kind of unity I mean. From all around this country, in fact, all over the world, these displays of compassion are being offered to one remote, small community in the middle of the cow pastures and the families that love them; a place most had never even heard of before Monday, but now, no one will ever forget.

I wish it did not take tragic events like this to bring people together. I wish the love and brotherhood did not fade away with time. Still, for the brief time that it lasts, it is like a glorious sunset. It is an awesome sight and you do not want to miss a minute of it. Watching this beautiful display of God's love and beauty, it is possible for me to believe that what evil meant for our harm, God is using for our good.

April 23, Flowers

"Delight yourself in the LORD,
and He will give you the desires of your heart."
- Psalm 37:4

It has been at least 15 years since I last saw my friend Caren. In fact, we lost touch for about nine years after we both moved. I was sad to lose contact with her, but accepted the fact that sometimes friendships are for a season, and felt grateful for the many ways God had used this beautiful woman in my life. She was an inspiration to me and I knew I would never forget her.

I discovered that our season of friendship was not over when we were reunited. Our daughters actually reconnected first through the Internet and eventually brought us back together. We kept in touch by phone and email for over a year and I really enjoyed having her back in my life.

I had hopes of seeing Caren again one day, but did not expect it to be any time soon since we lived so far apart and finances were a hindrance. Therefore, I was very surprised and excited when she contacted me to say she was coming to visit me. Her son had asked what she wanted for her birthday and she said she wanted a plane ticket to come visit me. I felt so special. Of all the things she could have chosen and she chose to see me. Wow!

I readied one of the girls' rooms for Caren to stay and made plans to drive to the airport to get her. When the day finally arrived, it occurred to me as I was driving to the airport that it would have been so nice if I had gotten some flowers to put in the room where Caren was staying. I know that she loves flowers and it would have added a cheerful, welcoming touch that she would have genuinely appreciated. I regretted that I had not thought of it sooner, but had no time to stop for them now. Within five minutes of that thought, I got a call from my daughter Hannah. She wanted to let me know that our neighbor had just stopped by to bring a beautiful arrangement of flowers. I was stunned. A coincidence? If so, it was an amazing one to me, but I did not believe it was. In the eight years that have known this neighbor, she has never brought us flowers.

I felt an overwhelming sense of God's personal love for me which brought me to tears. It was just a little thing, I know. I had not, in fact, even asked for it. It seemed to me, however, as if He was saying, *"I heard you wanted this and I just wanted you to know how special you are to me and how much I love you, so I sent you some flowers."* It got me to wondering how many gifts God has sent to me along the way that I have missed in my pre-occupation with myself. Fortunately, I did not miss this one, and they were the loveliest flowers I've ever received.

May 5, Trust

"Trust in the LORD with all your heart
and lean not on your own understanding."
- Proverbs 3:5

Recently, a friend confided in me that her husband did not trust her. She has been a faithful, loving wife for many years, and yet, he suspects she would cheat on him and possibly leave him for another man if she had the chance. She has never given him any reason to feel this way; in fact, she is very careful never to give the wrong message to other men. Her husband's doubt is not about her at all, but about his own insecurities and fears. She shared with me how difficult this is for her - to be trustworthy but not to be trusted. I understand her frustration, since it seems ridiculous that her spouse could doubt her.

I have another friend that I love very much. We have been friends for years and we have been through much together. She has walked with me through these past eight years of floundering in my blindness, and, while I rarely heard God's voice during that time, her reassuring voice gave me such comfort, knowing that I was not alone in my dark place, but she was right beside me. Lately, however, she has seemed more withdrawn from me. It seems that she has been doubting my love for her and I feel like I have to be careful what I say or she will retreat from me. I am still here for her as I always have been, but she does not seem to trust me as much anymore.

Pondering these two cases, I identified my tendency to do the exact same thing to God. All my life, He has been there, loving me faithfully. Yet, I have never fully trusted Him. I have frequently doubted His love for me. I have feared that He would hurt me. I have accused Him and withdrawn from Him. In my fear of His rejection, I have rejected His love, just as my friend's spouse is rejecting her love and my other friend is rejecting mine. It is not because I do not want it. I desperately do. It is just because I do not trust God - because I am afraid to trust. These two friends have helped me to see just how that feels from the other side.

I do not want to hurt God anymore or allow the enemy to continue to rob me. I want to fully receive the awesome, unconditional love that God offers me. My insecurities do not change one thing.I am loved and always have been.

May 7, The Monster

It's like this huge, horrible monster that comes along and swallows me whole. One day, I am fine, the next I am trapped and helpless inside this beast. I can still see, but not very clearly; everything is distorted. I feel out of control as it wreaks havoc on my life and my relationships; raging with anger, relentless criticisms, self-pity, and resentment. I get confused as I fall prey to its lies about others and myself. Depression and despair fall over me like a heavy wet blanket and I feel like I will suffocate under its weight. When the monster finally slinks away, I am left defeated and discouraged, full of self-loathing and sometimes lingering anger towards others who have lost all compassion for me in this ordeal; who, in their desire to stay as far away from the monster as possible, also have stayed far from me in my time of need. No one can hear me crying for help in here.

I call my monster PMS and that is my life once every month (at least). Some months it is blessed brief, just two or three days. On other months, it can be as long as a week or even two. Those months cause me to lose hope. To some people, I am sure this description would sound like a cop-out. That does not really matter because this is my journal and I understand exactly; as I am sure any other woman with PMS would as well. No worry of me giving myself a pass or being too easy on myself. No, that is one thing of which I have never been guilty; quite the opposite. I am a perfectionist, after all. I do not need any help beating myself up.

I remember years ago, when, as a young mother, PMS seemed to rule my life. I spent two full weeks every month absolutely devoured by this monster and two full weeks afterward, depressed over the wake of disaster it left behind. For a few years, there was no such thing as a "good time" of the month for me.

It was in this desperate state that I attended a prayer meeting at my church one night. We were invited to come up for prayer with the deacons and their wives. As I was standing in line thinking that I did not want to have to tell one of these male deacons my very personal, very female problems, our pastor suddenly interrupted the service. *"Let's change this - let's have the deacon's wives on one side and the deacons on the other. That way the women can go for prayer with the women and the men with the men."* I have no idea what his motivation was for that decision, but it was one of those moments when I felt like God had shifted the earth for me!

When my turn came, I shared with a group of women that included some of my closest friends, many of whom were fully aware of my dilemma. They laid their hands on me and poured out loving, heart-felt cries to God on my behalf. God healed me that night. I was instantly set free from this plague that had consumed my life.

For years, I no longer had a problem with PMS. Unfortunately, it eventually returned and I have again been wrestling with it for several years now. I have tried everything. Diet, exercise, herbs and natural supplements, even alcohol...anything I could think of that might help. Many of these things have been helpful. Certainly, when I am taking care of my body it makes a difference. Still, it is a demon I am always battling. Through this past month as I have experienced God's emotional healing and insights in my life, I have had more peace than I have had for many years. I breezed through my period last month as if it was nothing. No PMS at all.

I guess I was expecting that from now on I would just merrily float through life in constant harmony. If I bring every need to God, He will meet it, right? That was my hope and that is what I have been doing. Then, when I started feeling a little irritable a few days ago, I prayed for God to change my attitude. I kept praying and it did seem to help, but it did not go away completely.

Yesterday, I woke up feeling blue and discontent. I just wanted to be left alone, but this was our family day. Since that was my idea, I could not just bail on it. I went into my bathroom and pleaded with God. I was beginning to be suspicious that the old monster was creeping back. I struggled with the fear that I had not changed at all; that my family would be disappointed in me once again, thinking that it was just another one of my "phases" that did not last. I wondered how I could continue to share with others what great things God is doing in my life when it seems that I am still in bondage to my weaknesses. If I were honest about where I am now, the hope that I had offered others might seem meaningless.

God did bring some relief to me and I was able to enjoy some pleasant time with my family later in the day. Today, however, I woke up even more depressed, not wanting to face the day. Again, I prayed and rebuked the enemy's attacks. I realized that, while I could ask God to deliver me, I must accept, as Jesus did, that it may not be His will. I made the decision to hold onto God even if I have to walk in darkness again.

I thought about the times when one of my children has come to me with a wound. I have to clean the wound even though I know it will cause them more pain. I do not like to do this, but I know it is necessary in order for the wound to heal properly. My kids allow me to do it because they trust me; they know I want only what is good for them. With this image in mind, I decided to try really hard to sit still and let God clean my wound even though it really hurts and I would much rather He just magically made it disappear - maybe with a *Barney* band-aid or something.

I have spent enough years questioning God. I will try something different this time. I will try believing. I will try submitting. I do not have to panic and assume that, because I hurt, God has left me. When life gets hard for my kids, they run *to* me, not away from me, because they know that I am always here for them. They know that I am **for** them. It is time for me to learn that my Father is not just here for me in the easy times, but is here for me all the time. God is **for** me.

May 8, Happy Birthday to Mom

Today is my Mom's birthday. She would have been 71. I lit a candle on "her" table and sang Happy Birthday, as is my tradition. Remembering her birthday this year is gratitude and sadness for me at the same time. I am thankful for the mother God gave me and for the 36 years that she was here for me. I am sad that she cannot be here now to share my life and see her grandchildren grow up into the lovely people she knew they would become.

It seems to me that at this point in life, the relationship between mother and daughter could be the most enjoyable. I have grown up some from my arrogant youth; I have raised my own children long enough to appreciate what a difficult task it is and be uninclined to be critical of any of my mother's mistakes. God has humbled me and I have softened. I have also been learning what my mom always tried to teach me - to lighten up and enjoy life, to take care of me because I matter too. Mom would be happy about that. How wonderful it would be to have her here to do some of that enjoying with me. Then again, Mom is in a better place now and I would not want to change that.

I will have to content myself with the many wonderful memories of her. I remember her beautiful voice; she could sing like an angel and I have no doubt she has a prominent place now in God's heavenly choir. One of my favorite songs to hear her sing was *"Sentimental Journey"*, especially when she sang it with her sisters. They were terrific. There was nothing more soothing to me than laying my head in her lap while she caressed my hair and sang to me.

I will also never forget my mom's unconditional love, which was evident on so many occasions but never more clearly than the time I had the bright idea to run off to Texas with some boy I had just met and with whom I thought I was in love - I was 19. That must have been terrifying for her. Yet, when I came back a month later with my heart broken and my tail between my legs, Mom never said a single word that sounded remotely like *"I told you so"*. Without a hint of reprimand for my foolishness, she just took me in her arms and welcomed me home. That kind of love was exactly what I needed and it had a powerful healing effect.

When I was a young mother, Mom was always worried that I never took time for myself or did anything for me. I was so busy caring for my family that I had no time for that. I thought my resources would never run out (Boy, was I wrong!). So whenever Mom came to visit, she always made a point of pampering me - whether it was taking me out to eat, shopping, going to the movies, babysitting the kids so that my husband and I could go on a date or just trying to lighten my load by doing housework and cooking for me. It took losing her to finally understand her point and realize that, since she was not around to take care of me anymore, it was time I started taking care of myself - for myself and for my family.

That was my mom - a beautiful, vibrant woman who loved life and lived it to the fullest. She was the most giving person I know, always sharing whatever she had with everyone. She used to tell my sister and me that she was spending our inheritance on us while she lived and she did. What a special way to pass your assets on to your children. She was so positive and determined to be happy no matter what her conditions. She was a successful businesswoman and a hard worker. Whatever she wanted, or needed, she went after it with 110%. She was fiercely loyal and devoted to her family and friends and made every effort to be there for each of us. Everywhere she went in her many travels, Mom made lifelong friends. Everyone loved her because it was obvious that she loved people and made each one feel special.

I do not think I had any idea how many lives she had impacted until the day of her funeral. The huge crowd that attended and all the strangers who approached me with stories of how she had touched their lives overwhelmed me. People came from all over the country. I was so very proud to be her daughter.

It is for these reasons and many more that I honor my mother. I thank God for giving me the mother who was just right for me and for all He has taught me through her love and her life. I will miss her until the day I die. Still she lives on...in me, in my sister, in her grandchildren, in the hearts of all of us who love her, and just possibly in the spit-fire spirit of a little great niece who carries her name.

May 11, Mother's Day

Mother's Day is almost here. Time to be showered with gifts, cards and pampering. Time for our families to stop the demands on us for a day and appreciate all that we do for them. After all, we deserve it, right? We are giving to and caring for them all year long. They should be grateful.

Then again, where did I get the idea that my family owes me gratitude? Is appreciation something I can demand? Well, I will admit, I have certainly tried at times and I can say for sure it does not work. I can demand all I want, but they appreciate me or they do not. Maybe it is time for me to stop thinking about what I deserve and instead remember all that God has blessed me with that I do not deserve at all.

Therefore, I am going to do something different this Mother's Day. My mother is not here to appreciate and thank. However, God has put other women (all wonderful mothers) in my life for which I can be grateful. I am going to let each of them know how much they mean to me.

Here's another thought. There are five people in my life, without whom I would ever have had the privilege of being called *mother*. That is a gift. Many women cannot have children; others struggle with sick children; then there are those who are grieving for lost children. I am very blessed among women. I think my children are awesome. Each one of them has their own unique personality and their own unique relationship with me. I treasure every one of them. Therefore, this year, I am going to let each of them know that I celebrate the gift they have given me of motherhood.

Mothers are a great gift and it is right that we honor and appreciate them. For me this year, however, as God continues to humble me in every area of my life, I want to take the opportunity of Mother's Day to remember not what I give, not what I am "owed", but what I have. And give thanks.

Chapter 3

Abiding

May 15, My Grace is Sufficient

"To keep me from becoming conceited, I was given a thorn in my flesh, a messenger of Satan, to torment me. Three times I pleaded with the Lord to take it away from me. But He said to me, 'My grace is sufficient for you, for My power is made perfect in weakness.' "
- 2 Corinthians 12:7-10

I have been asking God to heal me from PMS but, so far, He has not chosen to do so. He does, however, seem to be answering my prayers to keep the monster at bay. By His power, with much prayer, I have been overcoming my battles with issues such a depression, anger, critical thoughts, and self-pity. This past week, though, I have felt very blah. I have no energy or motivation. I do not want to talk with anyone or do anything. I would like to just go back to bed and stay there all day. Nonetheless, I cannot. I am a mom. There are no vacation days or sick days from motherhood. I will have to stumble through and hope I can keep my big mouth shut. Only by His grace.

The thought of continuing to spend my life in this monthly struggle is discouraging to me. It is like a cloud that returns repeatedly to hover, taking all the sunshine out of life and turning my world from vibrant colors to grays. I suppose it would be unrealistic of me to think that life can always be blue skies. Yet, even in the midst of it, God continues to teach me. I do not want to make the mistake I have made so many times of thinking that God does not walk with me through the tough times. Therefore, I am making a choice to believe He is with me, carrying me, and working all things out for my good, even PMS.

Paul talked about the thorn in his life that was there to keep him from becoming conceited. Though he pleaded with God to take it away, His answer was *"My grace is sufficient for you"*. PMS seems to be my thorn. In spite of the many ways in which God has humbled and convicted me, I can see how very easily I could become proud and take the credit for what He has done in me. So maybe I need a thorn. His grace IS sufficient for me. As in all things, God's way is superior. So I submit. *Let Your will, not mine, be done, Lord.* Even through PMS, I find relief in this letting go. I am so tired of squirming and resisting, and it feels good just to accept and let God worry about it.

May 30, Surrender, Again

> *"Submit yourselves, then, to God.*
> *Resist the devil, and he will flee from you."*
> - James 4:7

It has been awhile since I have wrtten. I guess I have not had much to say. No, that's not true. I just have not felt like saying it. I looked back at my journal and saw that it has been about two weeks since I wrote about my ordeal with PMS. I kept waiting for things to get better, for my joy to return. It has not. As suddenly as I found myself lifted up to the mountaintop, I was plunged back down to the valley. I am still sore from the fall. It is much easier to write about the mountaintop experiences. They make everyone feel good and give us hope. I guess I have hated to even admit where I am right now because I did not want to discourage others who have been encouraged by what I have shared in the past. However, we cannot live on the mountaintop all the time if we are to grow. It seems there is much more to learn in the valley anyway and, though it has been painful, God has continued to work in my heart in so many ways. Besides, it is important for me to remember my entire journey and not just the pleasant part.

One morning recently I woke up with the thought, *"The devil knows exactly how to defeat me and that is just what he is doing."* I do not normally wake up with such thoughts and I felt sure it must be from God. It is important to be aware so that I am not deceived. The most vulnerable areas of my life are my marriage, my family and my physical health. I have been under attack in all of them. Recognizing this was helpful. Still, after years of my effort to overcome my problems, I have learned my lesson. I am finally convinced that only God can deliver me. I needed to surrender it all to God **again** and rely on Him to work it all out. Surrender my hopes, dreams, frustrations, fears, doubts. Once again, just let go and place myself in His gentle arms. Easier said than done, for sure and I have had to do it repetitively, but it is also a great relief. My shoulders are not strong enough to carry it all.

As I yielded, God showed me how I have again been slowly turning back to counting on others instead of Him. It was such a subtle shift and I did not even see it happening. Yet, it was then, as I took my eyes off myself and put them back onto Jesus, that I was blindsided by an insight that should have been obvious to me long ago - but it was not. I realized that, in my selfish desire to be loved by my husband, I have not considered that his need to be loved by me might be greater. I have pushed him away more times than I would like to admit. This thought shamed me. I repented and prayed for a change my heart. Since then my husband has been at his most annoying. God has a sense of humor. But, hey, this is God's work and I am done with straining to "be like Jesus" - as if I ever could. I will just sit back and watch Him work. Actually, it may not always be pleasant, but it sure is freeing.

May 31, Where Did I Go Wrong?

"He who began a good work in me will be faithful to complete it."
- Philippians 1:6

Maybe it is typical to wrack your brain trying to figure out what you have done wrong when you are not experiencing easy fellowship with God. It is typical of me, anyway. For weeks now, I have pleaded with God, *"What happened? Show me what went wrong; what I need to change? What did I do wrong, God? What didn't I do that I should have?"* Maybe I am not praying enough (I cannot believe I could still fall for that old snare!), so I tried to pray more and my prayers were such an effort. Gone was that natural, easy interchange I had been having with God for these past months. What happened to His Presence that I had felt flowing through me, making loving and giving to others so easy?

Even in this frustrating time, though, I have still recognized a difference in me. Maybe I have not felt peace and joy, but I have felt trust. I have felt loved. I have not felt alone. I have doubted myself, but I have not doubted God.

Now that is nothing short of a miracle! It is something that God has accomplished in my life that I can hold on to. And I do. It has gotten me through some difficult weeks and helped me to believe that what I experienced was real.

It then dawned on me the other day that all this concentration on what I had done wrong was ridiculous. How thick is my skull and what will it take for God to get this message through to me? It is not about me, remember? It is not about what I do or do not do. It is God's good work, not Avery's. **He** will complete it! Been there, done that, and yet I still keep trying to go back for another visit. Thank God it is not about what I have done (wrong or right). So back I go - just believe, yield, rest. Everything else is His job. Good deal. I will get this eventually, I suppose.

June 1, This Little Light of Mine?

> *"I am the Vine; you are the branches...*
> *apart from Me you can do **nothing**."*
> - John 15:5

I am slowly beginning to understand a little about what it means to "abide"(or live) in the Lord. Jesus did not tell us to imitate Him. Our job is not to generate life, but to receive it from Him, allowing God to live through us. Therefore, in casting my cares on God instead of obsessing over them, I can find deliverance. After years of striving to imitate Jesus' life, this sounds easy enough.

This morning, I left the house early to run some errands. All the way in to town, I prayed, *"Let me abide in You today, Lord."* I went to the grocery store feeling optimistic. God was going to shine through me today! Everything was going great until I got to the deli section. There were two women behind the counter going about their business. I was apparently invisible. Having experienced this before at this deli, it did not take me long to feel irritated by the way they seemed to be blatantly ignoring me. Yet the final straw occurred when another customer walked up and they immediately offered to help her. I'm thinking - this is a joke, right? I looked around for a mirror to make sure that I was indeed visible. Then I called out to one of the deli women while waving my arms, *"Yoo-hoo! Do you see me? I'm here!"* Yes, I am embarrassed to say that I really did do that. She casually replied that she would be right with me - sure, as soon as she finished waiting on the customer who arrived after me. I rudely replied, *"Well, I was here first."* I immediately felt ashamed of my conduct and silently asked God for forgiveness though I could not bring myself to apologize to the deli woman. She would probably think I was nuts, I justified. Pride is such an ugly thing. So much for abiding in Christ.

I then went to the Post Office. I had some books to mail and the clerk asked me if there was anything else in the first package besides a book. When I told her there was a card, she said she had to charge me double. I could have sent the card by itself for only 41 cents! It did not make any sense to me. When I gave her the second package, I was ready. *"No, just a book"*, I lied. I got the book rate. I walked out of the Post Office feeling guilty (again). Did I really just lie to save myself a couple of dollars? It struck me as funny and I started laughing. I love God's ironic sense of humor! Abiding, Spirit-filled Avery. Aren't I just a little light to the world?

I managed to stay out of trouble as I ran the rest of my errands. Actually, I was too busy laughing at myself to misbehave anymore. I understand that in the spectrum of human behavior, my misconduct was relatively minor. The point of this lesson for me is that even when I really wanted to do the right thing, I could not manage it. If there was any doubt left, this day has made it very clear to me that I cannot generate a Christ-like life, but must to depend entirely on Christ - every moment.

It is such a very difficult thing for a perfectionist to stop trying to be perfect and learn simply to rely on God. It takes a long time to undo this kind of performance-based mentality. God certainly has His Hands full with me. My prideful self will not be denied or die easily. That's ok, though, because God is eternally patient with me. It will be interesting to watch Him work. To be able to laugh at myself and recognize that I am loved and accepted anyway is freeing beyond belief.

I continued laughing all the way home and was still smiling when I pulled up to my house. I do not know if I realized it before, but God is a really funny "guy". (Can I say that about God? I just did.)

June 4, Childlike Faith

"Truly I tell you, anyone who will not receive the kingdom of God like a little child will never enter it."
- Mark 10:15

There was a time when a day of constant setbacks like yesterday would have left me feeling defeated and beating myself up. What a glorious testimony to His work in me that I was instead able to laugh at myself and accept my flaws. I can rejoice that God's Spirit dwells in me and welcome His grace. God is able even though I am not. I needed to try and fail at abiding on my own efforts to see that He is the only One who can keep me. Part of abiding is knowing that He can keep me even when I cannot keep myself.

I must depend upon God moment by moment. Thinking about this idea reminded me of how Jesus said we need to come to God as little children. I thought of when my own children were small. They relied on their father and me for everything - food, shelter, protection, even their happiness to a large degree. They did not worry about the future because they trusted us to provide for them. As I have said before, when they were hurt, physically or emotionally, they did not run **from** us, they immediately ran **to** us, completely trusting that we would know best how to care for them. They never questioned that Mommy and Daddy would always be there for them and know what to do in every situation. They were completely dependent upon us. As they grew older, that dependence decreased. They questioned us more; longed for more independence; wanted to take care of themselves. While this is a natural part of growing up, it is, unfortunately, also the way our response to God changes as we "grow up". Therefore, Jesus' statement makes perfect sense. We have to go back to that complete trust and dependence on God in order to experience the abiding relationship with Him. That is where we find the contentment for which we long. We make it so complex, but, in reality, it is so simple only a child can understand it.

June 10, What I Already Am

> *"...anyone who belongs to Christ has become a new person. The old life is gone; a new life has begun!"*
> - 2 Corinthians 5:17

I am learning that one of the greatest deceptions of the enemy is that I must work to become what **I already am** in

Christ. If he can convince me that I am responsible for my righteousness or else I will be hopelessly condemned to live a sinful life, then he has conquered me. The truth, however, is that in Christ I am already free from my sinful nature. That is a privilege that perhaps many Christians do not embrace. I know that I did not for a long time.

I am only recently recognizing how misled I have been. I have not understood that *"The One who is in me is greater than the one who is in the world"* (1 John 4:4). I have allowed my enemy more power in my life than he actually has. Satan would not want us to comprehend that Jesus has stripped him of his power. He has no power over me unless I give it to him. And, boy, have I! I have fallen for the same lies over and over for years. That is why I begin each day asking God to protect me from deceit and open my eyes to truth. As a result, I have been constantly amazed by the ways that prayer has been answered.

I am still not entirely sure how this abiding thing works but I am beginning to understand that oneness with Christ is not something I must obtain, but something that has already been given to me. *Experiencing* that oneness is another matter. That is where faith comes in. God has grown my faith over these past months in a way I have never before known. Still I do not always *feel* at one with God. The devil would like me to believe that I have to feel a certain way or I am not experiencing unity with the Lord. Another of his lies.

I have a tendency to let my emotions guide me and this sometimes gets me into trouble. God has been showing me that I cannot count on them and should not follow them. However, I can count on God. No matter how I may feel; whether flying high and feeling close to God or down in the dumps and feeling like He is miles away, He is always the same - right there with me. Since my relationship with Him has for years been dictated by my emotions, the best thing He can do for me is to teach me how to walk in faith with no emotional experience. This is a difficult adjustment for me, but learning to have confidence in God no matter what my feelings may be is comforting.

There is great peace in understanding **that I am who I have always been in Christ**, no matter what my enemy says, my emotions say or my behavior says. **God says** I am a new creation in Christ, the old has gone, the new has come. This happened, not the day I felt it or even understood it, but the day I accepted it. Now **that** is freedom!

June 12, Abiding

> *"Our sinful nature no longer controls the way we live.*
> *The Holy Spirit now controls the way we live."*
> - Romans 8:4

This is the week that the monster usually visits me. So far, I have not seen hide nor hair of her. I have spent years trying everything I could think of to get rid of this monster, but this time, I did nothing. I just prayed, *"Lord, I don't want PMS this month, but if you choose to allow it, I surrender to Your will and ask You to help me to learn whatever I need from it."* Period. (No pun intended.)

This is Avery on PMS - moody, touchy, resentful, depressed, angry, wanting to **be** cared for, anti-social. This is Avery now - joyful, peaceful, effortlessly giving even when it is unappreciated, wanting **to** care for, wanting to reach out. Let me be clear here that I am not bragging. Let me also clarify that this is **not** Avery. This could be only be that sweet, gentle Spirit that lately has been transforming my heart and my life. I am just sitting in the background going, *"Wow! This is unbelievable!"*

Who is this woman? I do not know her, but I have to say I like her much better than the Avery I know. I think this must be what is called abiding. It is humbling, exciting and absolutely amazing. I think I could get to like this. The best part is that my part is very easy and simple - just submit. And to be honest, I think even that much is God's achievement.

Chapter 4

Growing Pains

June 13, Growth the Hard Way

"Her children rise up and call her blessed."
- Proverbs 31:28

My mom died eight years ago today. It seems like a lifetime ago. Even though I knew she was dying, it was sudden and came as a shock. She had a brain tumor, but she died of heart failure from an infection that had over-run her weakened immune system. I had believed that I had at least a year left with her, but came back to the hospital after lunch one day to find that she was gone. There is never a good time to say goodbye to your mom, but I was not ready at all. I guess I never would be. It was probably the hardest day of my life. However, I am not the same person I was eight years ago and much of that change has come through the grief and growth that was a result of losing Mom. God has used that difficult time in my life to produce many valuable things. My mom always tried to look for the positive in every situation, so I know she would be glad about that. Thus, I am not grieving today. I will always miss my mom. Today, though, I am thankful for all that I received from my mom - in life and in death.

June 18, No Illusions

"Be merciful to me, O Lord, for I am in distress;
my eyes grow weak with sorrow; my soul and my body with grief.
My life is consumed with anguish and my years with groaning.
My strength fails me. But I trust in You, O Lord.
You are my God. My times are in Your Hands."
- Psalm 31:9-10, 14-15

I tried to plan a happy little family camping trip to celebrate Father's Day this past weekend, with visions of the wonderful bonding memories we would all cherish. It did not happen that way. My teenage daughters complained the whole time and my husband was in essence AWOL (i.e., emotionally unavailable). I did my best to hold my tongue, but I was deeply disappointed and hurt.

I have devoted my entire adult life in pursuit of building a loving, happy family environment, and yet, the result has lately been a hostile, critical, negative family life. I accept my share of the responsibility for this. I know I have plenty of shortcomings. I also understand that these are turbulent years for my teenage girls. Still, it baffles me. Even more, it breaks my heart.

This weekend, watching the way my kids talked to each other, their inability to just enjoy being together as a family and my husband's withdrawal, it was all just too much for me. I could feel myself withdrawing as well; could feel the old resentments coming back. By Sunday morning, when the girls were asking once again when we were going home, I told them to feel free to go. We had two cars with us, so by 9:30am, they were all packed up and ready to leave for home. I was actually relieved to see them go. I was also ready to go crawl in a deep hole and sob my heart out.

While my husband and son went off to play in the water, I stayed at the campsite. I just wanted some time by myself. By this time, I was in a serious funk and had no idea how to get myself out of it. I grieved all day; in fact, I cried myself to sleep last night. Then this morning, I began my day in tears and just kept going.

There are times when the hurt in my heart over my family is a physical thing. That is how I have felt since yesterday. I have certainly cried to God - but my heart remains heavy. I am dragging through this day unable to think clearly or motivate myself. I found myself revisiting some of the old familiar questions and fears. That is when I finally sat down and relinquished my burdens to God. It is discouraging to find myself in this place again. Still, I am where I am and I am not going to try to come up with some pat answer or some moral of the story. Sometimes life just hurts. I struggle to hold on to just one thing, if even by a thread: I am loved.

June 19, Sister Love

"So encourage each other and build each other up,
just as you are already doing."
- 1 Thessalonians 5:11

I feel much better today. I lost my focus for a bit there, but God has faithfully brought me back. He did it very simply through love. I can so easily get caught up and discouraged by my circumstances. When my eyes are on Jesus, no matter what life brings, it cannot beat me. Only they were not. They were on me.

God did not give me what I deserved. He gave me what I needed, showing me His tender compassion through my friends, who spoke such wisdom and encouragement to me. My sister reminded me that by the standards I was setting up, probably all of us mothers are failures - but we are not. Most siblings fight, she pointed out, just as she and I did, and now we are the best of friends. There is always hope for our children's relationships.

My friend Cheryl reminded me that dying to self is a daily process that will continue until..."*when we see Him, we will be like Him*" (1 John 3:2). My friend Caren shared with me that fruit only comes from those who are abiding in the Vine and we do not have the ability to make our children abide in the Vine. Only God can accomplish that. My friend Lori just happened to send me a beautiful music CD, which, as I listened, brought healing to my soul. I also remembered her comment that, though I may lose my way at times, I come back much quicker than I used to and that is a sign of God's transformation in my life.

All of my friends offered me empathy and understanding. As I reflected on these demonstrations of love, I realized what a gift it is to have such beautiful women as friends. How could I feel anything but grateful?

July 1, Rejoice With Those Who Rejoice

> *"Keep your eyes on Jesus, who both began*
> *and finished this race we're in."*
> - Hebrews 12:2

I was reminded today of a conversation I had with a friend about a year ago. She told me that whenever she was having a hard time, she knew it meant she needed to get her focus back on Jesus. My blunt, honest response was "*Whatever. That means nothing to me.*" Now I find myself saying the very same thing and realize how much God has recently made Himself so real in my life. I thought back to those years of despair when I felt so hopeless, believing my life would carry on that way forever. Then one day, God turned on the lights and I have not been the same since. I am astounded at the changes in my heart.

I started wondering how many people read when I write about keeping my focus on Jesus and say, "*Whatever, I have no idea what that means*" or "*That's great for Avery, but God will never do anything like that for me*". Some people tell me they wish they could have my faith. So do I. Yet I did not have "my" faith until God chose recently to give it to me. I get impatient with God sometimes for those longing for more faith, though I know that God does not love me any more than He loves any of His children. God's way of reaching each of us, however, is as unique and special as we each are to Him. No one else's experience will be just like mine. Still I do believe that God can and will meet the needs of every heart that seeks Him, in just the right way, in just the right time. I cannot wait to see God's amazing work in each of my loved ones lives. What a privilege that will be!

Chapter 5

Letting Go

July 2, Lunch With a Friend

I had lunch with a friend today. Imagine that. The funny thing I am learning about this God I am just lately getting to know is that He seems to enjoy giving me the desires of my heart - right after I release them. For the eleven years that we have lived here, I have desperately wanted friends, true friends (that lived closer than 400 miles away!). There have been possibilities and hopeful moments, but, for the most part, they have eluded me. Finally, a few months ago, I realized that I was looking for friends to meet the needs that God wants to meet in my heart. So I relinquished that desire. I made a decision to look to God for my friendship needs and accept whatever He did or did not give me in the way of human relationships.

I began to be more appreciative of the long distance friendships He has given me with some terrific women. Maybe it is a rare occasion when I can sit down and have a cup of coffee with any of them, but still they are always there for me. I get more from those friendships than most women have in a whole community of relationships. I became content with what God has given me.

About a month ago, my neighbor called and said she is starting a Thursday Morning Women's Club and wondered if I was interested. There would be two members - her and me! It sounded wonderful to me so we began meeting outside between our houses once a week for coffee and companionship. My neighbor has always been a precious friend to me though she is old enough to be my mother. However, until her recent retirement, we rarely spent time together. I find myself looking forward to Thursday mornings all week.

So back to my lunch with a friend. This past year, at our homeschool co-op, I became friendly with another mom. We had been talking about getting together, so I finally called her and we set a date for lunch. She suggested a little tea cafe that has an Indian flare and we sat in a curtained-off booth on cushions for chairs with a tray for a table. It was unique and fun. We had tea and lunch and talked for two and a half hours about everything. I felt so grown up; is this how other women live? Well, probably not most of us; not most moms anyway.

As I said goodbye feeling most content, it dawned on me that, when I finally stopped looking, God decided to give me the female companionship for which I had been longing. I felt loved. He knows. He cares. God wants me to put Him first, but He also wants to give me the desires of my heart.

Most of us women are desperately lonely and isolated from one another. We worry about impressing each other; measuring up; always thinking other women have it more together than we do. Yet really, we are all basically the same. We need each other. God understands that. After all, He made us that way.

July 6, Dying to Myself

"For to me to live is Christ, and to die is gain."
- Philippians 1:21

What does it mean to "die to myself"? I really do not exactly know. I do know that it hurts. **A lot**. I know that I am no good at it because myself does not want to die. I know that myself wants to be loved, considered, appreciated and respected. I know that myself does not like to be ignored or ridiculed. I also know that I have experienced disappointments in these areas on a regular basis. Perhaps dying to myself is about accepting that and letting go of my right to those things. If so, I feel sure this is not something I am able to do. Still, lately, I have become more aware of my reactions to such offenses and how very tightly I hold onto my "rights" and my "self".

If I am completely honest, I must admit that the idea of dying to myself scares me - to death (now that is ironic). Yet, I want it more than anything. The reason is simple. As long as myself is standing in the way asserting all her rights, it seems to me the Holy Spirit's ability to live and work through me is limited. I want all God has for me and I definitely do not want to stand in the way.

Jesus did not assert His right to be loved, considered, or respected, though He deserved it more than anyone ever has. He faced rejection and judgment with humility, kindness and forgiveness. He understood the secret of dying to oneself. Many Christians talk about following Jesus' example (i.e., *"What would Jesus do?"*). It seems to me that if we are to follow Jesus' example, then we would merely stop attempting to imitate Him and lean on God's strength. That sounds like an easy thing - like doing nothing. Yet I am learning that resting in the Lord is anything but passive. It is not at all easy. It is a minute-by-minute choice between a preoccupation with me and my issues or being centered on God. I do not want to be *like* Jesus; I want His life in and through me. Therefore, casting all fears aside, I boldly proclaim, *"Yes, Lord, enable me to die to myself. I'm as ready as I'll ever be. I'm as willing as I can be. Bring it on."*

July 12, In the Name of Christ

> *"Jesus replied, 'He that is without sin among you, let him cast the first stone at her'."*
> - John 8:7

I saw a bumper sticker today that said, *"Jesus, protect me from your followers"*. There was a time when a statement like that might have offended me. After all, I consider myself one of Jesus' followers. Nevertheless, I was not offended. I appreciated the ironic humor and, at the same time, recognized the sad reality in it. More importantly, I found myself sympathizing with the sentiment. How very much damage has been done in the name of Christ. It grieves me to think of the damage I have done in the name of Christ, especially in my haughty youth when I believed that I had all the answers. How many people did I unwittingly hurt or turn off by my self-righteous, judgmental attitude? How did I ever dare to think that I represented Jesus when I have been so full of me?

Jesus did not judge; He loved. In my earnest desire to lead people to Christ, I wonder how many I have actually put off. People were drawn to Christ when He lived here on earth. If we represent Him, then we too would naturally draw people to Him. It seems to me like the church has done more of the opposite; we have done much to give God a bad name to the world around us and I am afraid that many people share the sentiments expressed on that bumper sticker.

Though my pride is still much too large, I appreciate the ways in which God has humbled me. Had I been successful in all the endeavors of my life, I would never have come to see the importance of God's grace. I would have continued in my pursuit of perfection in **my** strength (with "God's help"), taking pride in and credit for all my accomplishments.

Most of us see failure as a negative. My perspective on that has changed. Failure has brought me to my knees, and therefore, it is a gift. Failure has also left me less apt to judge others and more compassionate about their weaknesses. Strange as it may sound, I feel blessed that I was not able to achieve my goal of the perfect Christian wife and mother, because I have discovered something so much better.

Since abandoning my involvement in organized religion years ago, I have experienced a great deal of judgment and rejection from fellow believers. It was very painful at first, but I deserved it. I was reaping what I have sown because I have judged others in the same way. I see now that, instead of judgment, instead of shunning, what we really need to offer is the **unconditional** love of Christ. *"Freely you have received; freely give"* (Matthew 10:8).

This, too, has been a humbling lesson for which I am so grateful. It has given me the ability to empathize with people such as this one with the bumper sticker. It has also caused me to want to put down my stones and just love my "neighbor". *"Now then, who are you to judge your brother or sister?"* (Romans 14:10). *"For in the same way you judge others, you will be judged"* (Matthew 7:2).

We are all in need of grace. My prayer is that when the owner of that bumper sticker meets me, he will find nothing to fear, but simply see Jesus.

August 8, Dog (tired) Days of Summer

I started this journal as a record of my spiritual and emotional journey. I did not intend to talk about my physical wellbeing. For the past month, however, that has been my consuming battle. I have been too tired even to write. It has been all I could do to keep up with just the basics of cooking, cleaning, errands, taxi-ing kids everywhere, etc. A trip to the grocery store is Mount Everest. No matter how much I sleep, it is not enough. I have had no energy to put into my relationships. I have been walking around in a fog, feeling numb and empty.

This summer has been difficult and I have missed the exhilarating days of the spring when God seemed to be giving me one insight after another. I have had to lay down my wish to be well and accept my situation as it is. It has occurred to me that perhaps God gave me that wonderful spring season to prepare me for this one. Rather than worrying that God has left me, as I have in the past, I have had confidence that this is all part of His good plan for me as well.

Some days it feels like I am back in that dark room again, but it is different this time. I can feel Him holding my hand and I am not afraid anymore. There are times I hurt, times I feel discouraged, times I feel so lonely, but then He gently reminds me that He is still here. I am never alone. This understanding is worth going through even the lowest valley.

September 6, Unconditionally Loved

"May you have the power to understand,
as all God's people should,
how wide, how long, how high, and how deep His love is.
May you experience the love of Christ,
though it is too great to understand fully.
Then you will be made complete with all the fullness of life
and power that comes from God."
- Ephesians 3:18-19

These past few months I have been exploring this idea of abiding in the Lord. What does that mean? How is it attained? I have written about some of my discoveries as I have grappled with this concept.

During the summer, I became so frustrated because I was not seeing the changes in my behavior that I hoped would occur as a result of learning to abide and trust in God. If I were abiding in the Lord, His fruit would be evident in my life, right? Then one day recently, a light bulb went on inside me. It occurred to me that, while my attention has been on my behavior as the important result of abiding, God's priority has apparently been entirely different. He showed me that His interest in me is not about my performance. His purpose in my abiding is intimacy with Him; to know Him; to experience His love, to live in His peace and joy. Not about what **I** should do for God; what **He** wants to do for me! After a lifetime of conditioning to see love as something one must earn, this is such a foreign concept to me. Does He really mean for me to believe that He simply wants to love me for myself, just as I am?

I became aware that I am still trying to win God's approval. He reminded me, yet again, that I do not need to try. I already have it. I always have. I also realized I am still trying to look good to others; to win their approval. Yet I do not need to do that either. It is ok for others to see that I am flawed; we all are. I certainly love better from a humble place than when I am on my pedestal. As I recognized these truths, I was able to take another step in receiving and understanding God's absolute, unreserved love for me. I am awed by it. He is slowly, patiently melting my heart.

September 12, My Little White Flag

Motherhood has been an especially painful endeavor in the past couple of months. Many times, I have wanted to share my experiences and feelings through this trying phase of parenting, but I must respect the privacy of my children. I have often seen parallels in the way I treat God and in my children's behavior. I have only five children; I have wondered at the heartache God must face at having millions of His children doubt His love, reject Him, blame Him, hurt themselves with bad choices, and take His gifts for granted. My love as a mother is far inferior to God's, but I can relate to these heartaches and it has caused me grief to see that I have been part of this doubt, rejection, and lack of gratitude toward a Father who has loved me with such patience. I only hope and pray that I can put aside my own agenda and love my children with even a measure of that magnanimous love.

My marriage is also going through a distressing period as we have suffered through growing pains and the pressures of parenting. I believe the answer to all my marriage issues is simple to comprehend, but much more difficult to live. I seem to be a slow learner, because, repeatedly, God gives me the same message: *"Fix your eyes not on what is seen, but on what is unseen".* (2 Corinthians 4:18) When I am able to do that, instead of fixating on my needs and my husband's imperfect love for me, then I am able to love him and accept what he has to give. Of course, as with everything else, this is something that God will have to bring about in my life.

Lately, surrender seems to be the word of the day for me. My little white flag is waving high. I have spent years of my life fighting - fighting for my health, physically and emotionally; fighting for my family; fighting for my marriage; fighting to be the person I want to be; fighting for spiritual growth; fighting, fighting, fighting. I told God recently *"I am just done fighting!"* It has gotten me absolutely nowhere. I cannot conquer any of these things. So I gave them up - surrendered every one of them to God (yet again). If God wants to give me success in any of these areas of my life, then He can and He will. If He does not, then I am sure that He will do what is best for me.

God does not need my help, and in fact, it has obviously been more of a hindrance anyway. The hardest thing in the world for a "doer" to do is to just "be". Nevertheless, I have exhausted myself with my own efforts and I am ready to try (or should I say stop trying). I will just "be". Accept and "be". The rest is up to God. De-ja-vu, huh?

Chapter 6

What Really Matters

September 18, Dear Michelle

To my daughter's friend, who just brought her first child into the world:

"Dear Michelle,
Congratulations! Welcome to the world of motherhood, the most rewarding, difficult and important job you will ever have. This is a joyful time in your life but also I know it can be intimidating to think of the responsibility you have just been given. You want to be the best mother you can, but they come with no instruction manuals. So, for what it's worth, I would like to share with you what I believe are the most important lessons that I have learned in 20 years of mothering - from my heart to yours. While I know that you must make your own way as a mother, I hope you can benefit, even if just a little, from my experience.
First of all, do not make the mistake of believing, as I once did, that God has handed you a bundle of clay with which you can create the person you choose. Your little boy is a unique creation of God and you do not have the power to change who he is. It is instead your job to love, nurture, protect and, most importantly, accept that special personality.
I have learned that I am not in control, much as I would like to be, of my children's lives or anything else for that matter. Therefore, the

greatest weapon I have in defense of my children is prayer. Of course, you will want to pray for God's blessing and protection on his life, but my favorite prayer for my children is that God will reveal Himself to them and that His will may be done in their lives. Since He knows so much better than me what they really need, I would rather trust Him with the answers than ask Him to apply mine. It is my sincerest hope that my children will come to truly trust in God's unconditional, unfailing love at a much younger age than I have. That is my prayer for you, too, as I honestly believe this is the only way to find true peace and strength to deal with life's rough seas.

There is an endless list of responsibilities as a mother - feeding, clothing, protecting, teaching, disciplining, etc. It can be an overwhelming burden at times, wanting to be and do everything for them. However, when it really comes down to it, what children need most is love and acceptance. Love covers a multitude of sins. While I have and will continue to make many mistakes as a mother, for my children to know that they are loved by me and that I will always be there for them is the greatest gift I can give them. If they are sure of my love, I believe that I have succeeded as a mother.

Last, but not least, while I am sure you want to give your "all" to your child, it is important not to lose "Michelle" in the role of "Mom". Take time for yourself and your interests. Do not lose sight of who you are and do not feel guilty to take care of your needs. They say you can be a much better mother if you take care of yourself and it is true. I did not listen to this wise advice and now, after 20 years, I am trying to find "Avery" again, whom I gave up totally in my role as wife and mother. It not only hurt me, but my family suffered for it as well. Do not make the mistake I made. You family is important, but you do matter, too.

They say your children step on your toes when they are young and on your heart when they grow older. While there is a great deal of truth to this, there is no need to fear it. It is through the challenges and heartaches of mothering that God can do the greatest work in our lives. I am so grateful for how God has used the humbling experience of raising my children to transform my life and heal my heart. And I would not trade it for anything.

You will make mistakes. Every mother does. Trust God to guide you through each day and He will give you what you need when you need it. Be the best mother you can be, but forgive yourself for your regrets. Trust the amazing motherly instincts God has given you. They will not often fail you. No one knows what is best for your child better than you do. I know you will be a wonderful mother because you will love your child with all your heart and there is no more powerful love than mother love.

Please know that I am always here if you need me to provide support and understanding from one mother (who has been there) to another. God bless you and your beautiful little boy.

All my love,

Avery

September 20, Finding Avery Again

Last week, for the first time in twenty-five years, I attended a drawing class at the local community college. I have always called myself an artist, but, since I began having children over twenty years ago, I have used my talent very rarely. So, this was long overdue. Everyone was excited for me, but as the time for the first class approached, I became increasingly nervous. What if I am no good? What if I don't have everything I need? What if I do not have what it takes? Do I really want to walk into a classroom full of strangers feeling like the "new girl" all over again? I suppose some of us never get over our apprehension of the first day at a new school. Our family moved a lot when I was growing up, so I had many of those experiences as a kid and some of those memories are a little traumatic. But I digress.

I signed up for this class to do something fun for me and I should have been looking forward to it. This is silly, I chided myself. I am a grown, confident (?) woman and I have overcome far greater challenges than this. *"Just relax and enjoy it,"* my husband said.

The real root of my problem, however, is that at this point in my life, I just want too badly to accomplish something to be proud of. So instead of just enjoying, I put pressure on myself and worried about the dreaded "f" word (not that word; the worse "f" word) - *failure!*

The hardest part of the class was walking in that room for the first time. The teacher had started a dialogue before beginning the class to warm things up, and I came in as students were answering her question. As I found a seat, she turned to me for my answer. *"What is the question?"* I asked, feeling put on the spot and wanting to hide somewhere. So much for discreetly slipping in. She explained that she was interested in our reasons for taking the class. Ok, that's an easy one. *"After years of raising kids, I'm trying to find 'Avery' again,"* I replied.

After that, the class went pretty well. I liked the teacher and felt I could handle her assignments...until we started drawing a still life. Hey, let's go back to those easy worksheets where you tell me what to do step by step, I silently shouted. I hate still-lifes! At one point, I considered throwing my pencil down and walking out. I was so discouraged with my work. Still I persevered, and when she told us to walk around and look at everyone else's work, I was greatly encourage to see that mine was just as good as any.

I know it does not matter how good my drawings are. I do not have to succeed. In fact, haven't I already learned that success feeds my pride and keeps me from depending on God? (Well, I do tend to have to keep revisiting the same lessons). What matters is that I took my first step in rediscovering myself and exploring the gifts God has given me that I may use in this new season of my life.

The season of intense mothering is coming to an end for me and, while I might have given up a little too much of myself, I do not regret that I gave my best to my family. I am sure there will be some scary steps as I timidly reach out into the world again, but it is actually kind of exciting to see what God has in store for me.

September 26, When I Grow Up

A friend of mine wrote a blog about her children's aspirations for when they grow up, to which she added her own goals. Some of us never do grow up. Many more of us might just get there near the end of our lives. A rare few attain a great depth of maturity in their later years, inspiring awe in the rest of us. I would like to be in the last camp, but for now, I know I am not so grown up yet, and I was inspired to do a little dreaming of my own.

When I grow up, I hope to discover the secret to a genuinely close relationship with my Savior and the faith never to doubt His love. I want to know what it means to be able to rely fully on God throughout each day with a calm spirit, rather than being tossed around by life's storms. I would like to be a blessing, not a burden, to others; most of all, to my family. I want to play with my grandchildren. I intend to be a friend to my children. I plan to have fun with my husband, traveling and exploring the world together. I would like to spend more time enjoying nature. I want to dance until dawn.

While I am very blessed to be able to call some of the most special women on earth my friends, I would enjoy having a girlfriend living close enough to me to go shopping with, invite for coffee, and with whom I can pour out my heart face to face more often than once or twice a year. I want to read, read, read, and never stop learning. I would love to have my own art studio, and paint and draw to my heart's content. I want to explore my love of alternative healthcare and use my knowledge to help others.

I have always dreamed of being a support to pregnant women, physically and emotionally. The opportunity to be part of the fascinating world of pregnancy and childbirth in some capacity would be an incredible opportunity. I aim to take many pictures and create scrapbooks to preserve precious memories. I have been teaching my children for years and I am a little burned out from it, but I am a teacher at heart so I know that in some capacity, I must continue to teach. I hope to be brave enough to take risks and try new things. I plan to eat, drink and be merry! Most of all, I intend to make the best of what life brings me, treasuring the blessings, accepting the challenges, growing from the heartaches. I have a lot to look forward to when I "grow up". Of course, I do not know if I ever will grow up completely. I suppose fulfilling some of these goals would be part of that process. It is a big list, so I should probably get started right away.

October 26, Mika-Maka

"Charm is deceptive and beauty disappears,
but a woman who honors the Lord should be praised."
- Proverbs 31:30

Today my maternal grandmother would have celebrated her 92nd birthday if she were still with us. She passed away eight years ago, just over a year after we lost my mother. We were very close, so it felt like losing a second mother. My grandmother grieved deeply for her oldest daughter. She used to say that a parent should never outlive her child and it seemed to me as though she literally died of a broken heart.

We called her Mika-Maka, a unique and special name for a unique and special lady. When her first grandchild, my cousin, was just a baby, Mika-Maka used to play "Piggy went to market" with her little toes. My cousin came to associate her grandmother with this game and began to call her "Piggy Went to Market"; only it came out sounding something like "Mika-Maka". The nickname stuck and all her grandchildren grew up calling her by it. In fact, everyone used it - all the family and even her friends.

Mika-Maka has probably been my greatest spiritual inspiration. Her sincere and personal faith went far deeper than merely attending church on Sundays. While I recognized this at an early age, it was not until I began longing for my own intimate relationship with God that I truly came to appreciate Mika-Maka's genuine love for her Maker. Mika-Maka was a prayer warrior and she prayed faithfully for her family. She began her days sitting in her bed with a cup of coffee and her devotional book. Anyone who was around was invited to join her. Some of my fondest memories are of times spent curling up with her as we read and prayed together. I still miss her so. I cannot wait until the day I can see her again and thank her for the difference she made in my life. The heritage she passed on to me is greater than any treasure this world has to offer.

My precious Mika-Maka was one of the most beautiful women I have ever known and God's grace clearly shined through her kind, gentle spirit. I aspire to be even half the woman she was. I may never be, but I do know the way...on my knees. Just like my Mika-Maka.

February 10, The Healing Touch of Fellowship

"God can do anything, you know—
far more than you could ever imagine or
guess or request in your wildest dreams!
He does it not by pushing us around
but by working within us,
His Spirit deeply and gently within us."
- Ephesians 3:20

I knew I was meant to go to this meeting. I was really feeling the need for the encouragement of being with other believers, but I had no idea of all that God could do in just one day. His timetable is so very different from mine, and while I am despairing over how slowly I seem to progress in my faith, my little mind cannot grasp the power He has to move mountains in an instant when He so chooses.

We were invited to a meeting at the home of a friend of a friend, where one of my favorite Christian authors was coming to speak along with a couple of his friends. Though we knew almost no one, my family was welcomed warmly when we arrived. It was a casual, laid-back atmosphere and we socialized for the first couple of hours before everyone sat down for an informal group meeting.

A man named Paul spoke about a book he had just written called *"The Shack"*. I had never heard of the book, though everyone else seemed to be familiar with it, but after hearing him speak, I decided I wanted to read it. I felt an immediate connection with Paul and appreciated his candor and humility. Through the whole meeting, I was holding back tears (for no reason that I could decipher). I later realized it must have just been the refreshment of getting a "cool drink" of fellowship after years alone in the desert.

As the meeting disbanded for dinner, I spoke to the couple sitting next to me. Having learned that they lost their daughter in the college shooting a year ago, I expressed my condolences, telling them how much all the grieving families have been in my prayers. I felt almost guilty as I shared with them that my daughter had also been there that day. They explained of the peace they had, knowing that their daughter was with the Lord. Thinking of my own daughter's claims to atheism, I knew that I would have had to live with the agony of doubt, and therefore felt grateful for God's infinite wisdom.

My husband had other plans for the evening, so I joined some friends for dinner, and to my surprise, Paul also joined us. Through the whole meeting, I had been thinking that I would love to share some of my spiritual struggles with him and hear more of what he had to say. I was thrilled that God chose to bless me with this opportunity and I was sure it was not by chance.

All the way to the restaurant, I peppered Paul with questions about his evidently close relationship with God. I asked him flat out if he walked consistently in the peace and joy of intimacy with God, and he said, *"Yes, most of the time."* I could see that it was true. This is what drew me to him. I expressed my frustration in fully actualizing this in my own life. He patiently answered my questions and challenges. He read between the lines and acknowledged my hurt and anger. I explained to him my concern with wasting time spinning my wheels in this pursuit of harmony with God. Paul told me that none of it is wasted time; it all has a purpose; you never go backwards, only forward. I shared with him the changes God brought to my heart last spring and the contentment and faith that I found; how I had been truly able to experience God's love for the first time in my life and commune so naturally with Him all day long. I described how I had experienced this for a few months and then watched it slowly slip away from me, confused and discouraged. I could do nothing to keep it, just as I had done nothing to achieve it.

Paul spoke to me about the danger of projecting forward and thinking that the way it is now is the way it will always be (Boy, am I guilty of that.). He said God is not in my visions of my future; He is here with me now. I acknowledged that this is where I need to be. I remembered the verse God has been constantly bringing to mind lately: *"Don't worry about tomorrow, for today has enough worries of its own"* (Matthew 6:34). Yet how often have I worried about my visions of a future that has never come to pass?

Paul helped me to realize that I do not need to ask God why anymore, because His reasons are so far beyond my understanding anyway. I perceived for the first time that God could have loving reasons for what He does in my life that I can never imagine. I do not need to know; I only need to accept His love for me. In that moment, it seemed God gave me a very personal glimpse of that love. The God of the Universe loves me enough to send this man all the way from Oregon to answer my little temper tantrum. Paul reminded me that God is listening and He does answer my prayers.

I am not a "respecter of persons" and I do not believe God is. Paul is just a regular person who wrote a book that people are going crazy over. I have not read it, but I like Paul; I like his gentle spirit and his openness. I like that his book's popularity has not gone to his head and he does not feel the need to impress anyone. However, I **love** what I saw in Paul and it is just what I want people to see in me - Jesus.

We got back to the meeting after dinner, and I was feeling full of God's love and encouragement. I walked into the first room of the house to meet a tired young mother. I have certainly been there, I thought. I knew that I had encouragement and lots of understanding to offer her. This was just where I needed to be, so I sat right down and we shared like old friends for the rest of the evening. This was a day I will never forget, but more importantly, this was a life-changing encounter.

February 14, Marriage Is...

Marriage is...laughing together, crying together, grieving together, celebrating together, working together, growing up together, sometimes growing apart, fighting, hurting, rejecting, accepting, betraying, forgiving and being forgiven (70x70x70), loyalty, doubting, trusting, believing in someone you know will let you down, agreeing, disagreeing, taking, giving, standing by someone even when you dislike them, communicating, not communicating, security, insecurity, feeling love, feeling hate, feeling nothing at all, knowing there is one person in the world who truly knows who you are and loves you anyway, being one and yet separate, the hardest human relationship in the world and yet the most worthwhile... commitment.

Chapter 7

Real Life Struggles

February 16, Midlife Crisis

Is this what they call a midlife crisis - what I'm going through lately? In just a few short months, my homeschooling career of 16 years will be over. As much as I love having my sweet boy home with me, I am more than ready to put the books away and move on to the next phase of my life. Yet what is the next phase of my life? What will I be doing? The prospects, while exciting, are also a bit scary.

I suppose what gives me apprehension for the future is once again this sense of failure over the past. I have been a very involved mother. I have devoted all of my life to my family. I wanted to do my very best to be a wonderful wife and mother and successfully raise a family. While, as I have mentioned before, I am grateful for all the lessons that my failings have taught me, it does make it hard to look back and take stock of the past twenty-one years of mothering and homeschooling.

Again the doubts come. Would my kids have been any worse if I had sent them to school and had a life and career of my own? Have I really produced anything positive in their lives by my sacrifice? Would they have been better off if I had not been such an involved mother? Have I been pointlessly trying to teach children who are not receptive to what I have to offer? What have I really accomplished? Does my family really appreciate the sacrifices I have made for them? Or do they just resent the mistakes I have made and the ways I have failed them? Have I been wasting my life?

Lately, I have been feeling taken for granted; complaints rather than complements about my meals, being left to eat alone after I have served everyone else, messes left for me to clean up, muddy shoes trampling through a floor I have just mopped, dishes and clutter left all over the house with the unspoken expectation that I will take care of it all. Cleaning up after a family of perfectly capable people is not enough for me anymore. I cannot find any satisfaction in a day full of mindless jobs that I will just have to repeat tomorrow. I need more purpose in my life. There was a time when my family was young and they needed me, but, at this point, there is nothing I do for them that they cannot do for themselves.

It is time for me to move on in my life. I know this will be hard for my family and for me. They might begrudge the fact that I am not always there anymore. I will have to fight the guilt. However, I have served my family for a long time. I have done my best and given them my all. I refuse to live the rest of my life vicariously through them. It's my turn.

So..."*forgetting what is behind, and straining toward what is ahead, I press on...*" (Philippians 3:13).

February 25, The Bondage of Fear

> *"For God has not given us a spirit of fear,*
> *but one of power, love, and sound judgment."*
> - 2 Timothy 1:7

I am finally reading *"The Shack"* and it is a beautiful, powerful story. The conversations between Jesus and the main character really speak to me. I see myself in Jesus' descriptions.

Jesus explained to the main character in the book that his projections into the future are always dictated by some kind of fear and his desperate attempts to control it. He is trying to control something that is not even real; trying to play God. This all comes down to a lack of faith, not really believing deep in his heart that God truly loves him. Isn't this exactly what Paul, the author, was so gently trying to tell me?

Again it seems to come back to trust. So much, if not all, of my worries come from a lack of faith. This is why I believe God has been reminding me almost daily to take one day at a time. Being aware of this, I have seen so many examples of things I worry about that never even happen. I have spent so much of my life stressing out for nothing.

My feelings sometimes cause me to doubt God. Yet I know deep down that no matter how confused my fearful soul may become at times, I must hold on to the truth. Slowly and gently, God is loosening my tight little fist. As it begins to open, I am gradually able to release control and receive more of the endless gifts He has for me.

February 28, Caring Too Much

This morning it occurred to me that, for the past nine years, I have been constantly bombarded by the negativity of teenage daughters. It has taken its toll. This realization came in the midst of one daughter's particularly negative phase, after listening for days to complaints of her miserable life.

This is a regular part of my life and I hate it with a passion. It has only served to feed the discouragement and sense of failure that has plagued me. I know that it does not matter what I say in response; it will be wrong, and they are sure that I have no idea what it is like to suffer the way they do. Somehow, whatever the problem, I am at least partly to blame and I am supposed to fix it. And I have tried. For too many years, I have attempted to spare my children pain; tried to secure their happiness. Yet I never could; I never can. Actually, it is not my job.

This is not to say that I do not care - quite the contrary. I care too much. What my children cannot possibly understand until they are mothers themselves is that every burden they carry is mine as well. Every disappointment, every fear, every failure, every heartache, I carry as if it were my own. I even carry some for them that they do not yet see. Unfortunately, it does not end when they leave home. I believe it is a cross every loving mother carries for her children as long as she lives. I can understand the wisdom in keeping yourself out of the middle of your grown children's problems. When they are in your care, you often have no choice, but backing off as they grow up might be essential to your sanity. At least it is for a mom like me.

This morning, the unhappiness of my children overwhelmed me and I sobbed with utter grief. I do not know if my family is typical or not, but my children have experienced a great deal of unhappiness and loneliness in their short lives. The frustration of being powerless to change that has been unbearable to me. I cling like a life raft to my eldest daughter's newfound peace and happiness. It gives me hope for the others. I know that life cannot always be happy;

there are ups and downs. Yet, somehow, it is so much easier to accept this for myself than for my children.

As in so many aspects of mothering, I discern the parallel between my grief for my children and God's grief for His. How much of my relationship with God is centered on listening to me gripe about my misery? I know just how He feels. Though He is not powerless as I am, if He has truly given me a free will, He must allow me to make my choices, wise or foolish, and live with the consequences, not only of my own choices, but those of others as well. I am beginning to understand how hard that must be. There is much to be learned from God's style of parenting.

I turn to God in my despair over my own children and He reminds me that they are His children first. I recognize that their wellbeing in life is a load that I cannot handle and I understand that it is **not** too big for God. It is His to carry and He does not expect me to try. Once again, I see the need to count on Him; that, as great as my love is for my children, His love is far beyond what I have to offer them. I will probably take it back a thousand times, but for now, I give my burden to God. I know that is where it belongs. That does not make it any easier. They are part of me and they always will be. Then again, I guess He knows that.

March 18, At the End of My Rope

"You are blessed when you are at the end of your rope.
With less of you, there is more of God and His way."
- Matthew 5:3

After crying myself to sleep, I did not think I had any tears left, and yet, I practically woke up crying this morning. I poured out my heart to God, asking Him for comfort. It felt like my heart was breaking - again.

In a way, I have been grieving lately. On this morning, I felt too much despair to face the world. Before I even got out of bed, however, God began to convey to me exactly the message that I needed to hear.

God reminded me that He never wanted me to trust others. He wants me to love others but to trust in **Him alone**. We tend to expect that trusting God means counting on Him to make our lives easy and pain free. Then, when difficulties arise, we begin to question God's love. Yet, it is the painful circumstances that actually teach us to depend upon God. When things are going well, it is tempting to believe we can do it ourselves, forgetting our need for God. When our trust in God is based on our circumstances, it can be easily blown around by the winds of life.

So, actually, I am blessed. Coming to the end of my rope is really just coming to the end of me. It may not feel good. I may not like it. Yet, in truth, it is a good thing. It is also a comfort to know that I am right where God wants me...at the end of my rope.

March 23, Peace with God

My dad arrived yesterday to visit us for Easter and we decided to go to an Easter service today. No one else in the family wanted to go so it was just the two of us. I let Dad choose the church where he would feel most comfortable. I was looking forward to dressing up, singing Easter songs and taking communion to celebrate the best holiday of the year. I went with an optimistic attitude.

There was a little baby girl sitting in front of us in her pretty Easter dress, who made a lot of noise. For some, that is a great irritation. I thought about the message sometimes given to children in church - that God does **not** want to hear you. I was thinking the truth is probably quite the opposite; that God probably enjoys the playful sounds of a child far more than the grumblings of the adults who feel they are being cheated of God's message by the distraction of that "annoying child". Personally, I was enjoying the little girl's joyful noises unto the Lord.

As the service began, an insight struck me so powerfully that my heart beat faster and swelled with emotion. Out of the blue, it occurred to me that *I am at peace with God.* Perhaps as never before, I believe I honestly am at peace with God. My emotions threatened to get the better of me and I feared I would start sobbing in the middle of this quiet room full of strangers. I am not exactly at peace with my circumstances or my relationships. However, I can finally acknowledge that there is no connection between my problems and God's love for me. I find that I am no longer wavering in my confidence in God, depending on how well life is going for me. How much He loves me is not determined by how happy I am! This is not an easy time in my life. My burdens keep me up at night and at times overwhelm me. Still I am not blaming God anymore or expecting Him to make it all better. I am confident that He will use all these things for His glory and for my good. I am able to believe that He loves me through it all. I am actually, genuinely at peace with God! How cool is that?

March 24, Lessons From a Sermon

I went to the Easter service yesterday expecting nothing more than to enjoy the singing and some quiet time with the

Lord. Every word of the entire service was written in the program. No surprises. Yet, right at the start of the service, God made it clear that He could speak to me here as well as anywhere else. I was feeling elated and open to anything else God might have for me. As I said, I had no expectations. I knew that I was not there to meet my needs. I was there for my dad, and I was there to worship God.

When the time came for the sermon, I listened carefully and kept an open mind. I am not a big fan of canned sermons, but wisdom has come from stranger places. Imagine my shock when the minister began to preach about the very ideas God has been revealing to me. He said (and I quote), *"Freedom is found when you let go of expectations."* He went on to expound on this idea of letting go of our expectations - of God, of others, of our circumstances, of the past. He also spoke of forgiving. I had to smile as I listened. It seems when God wants to get a point across to me, there is no limit to the resources He will use. He speaks to me everywhere. Even in church.

March 25, Letting Go of My Rope

I did not sleep much last night. I lay awake for hours, feeling crushed by my burdens. I tried not to think. I tried to pray. Nothing helped. Finally, I decided to visualize handing over each of my burdens to God. I pictured myself lifting up a large bundle and God reaching down to take it from me. However, when I tried this with some of the bundles, they were far heavier than me, and not only was I unable to lift them, they were on top of me, squashing me flat. I envisioned God reaching down and lifting one off me, only to have another, even heavier one, take its place. God lifted each one from me, until finally they were all gone.

I did feel a little lighter after this exercise, but I still could not sleep. I felt as if I were drowning in my problems. I began to picture myself in a sea of faces, all shouting at me. I was holding on to the end of my rope to keep myself from going under. Then I thought, *"Why am I holding on? Wouldn't it be much easier to let go? Wouldn't it feel better to stop straining? Wouldn't it be a relief to die?"* So I released my rope. Then I began to sink. Once below the surface, all the noise and chaos stopped. I was floating down to the bottom of the sea, and it was calm, quiet and easy. It was a wonderful relief. I totally relaxed and allowed myself to sink all the way to the soft sea floor. I felt warm, safe and comforted there, and I found rest. That is the last thing I remember before I drifted off into a peaceful sleep.

Chapter 8

His Way, Not Mine

May 9, The Pure Joy of Pain

> *"Consider it pure joy, my brothers and sisters,*
> *whenever you face trials of many kinds,*
> *because you know that the testing*
> *of your faith produces perseverance.*
> *Let perseverance finish its work*
> *so that you may be mature and complete,*
> *not lacking anything."*
> - James 1:2-4

I have spent too much time ranting at God for allowing bad things to happen, equating my happiness with His love, and feeling rejected by Him whenever He has allowed me to suffer. It has recently been occurring to me that the main priority of my life has been my own happiness. I was only willing to accept from God those things that I considered "good", but resented those things that I considered "bad". This has only prolonged my pain as I have continually worked to fix my problems rather than releasing them to God.

In my stubborn determination to be self sufficient, I had to become totally exhausted with my own efforts before I was finally ready to rely on God completely. I am so grateful that God allowed my attempts to meet my own needs to fail or I would have continued to resort to them.

It is not that I believe God wants me to suffer. It is just that He knows this is the only way I will come to lean on Him. He is not willing to allow my efforts at saving myself to work, and therefore, have me settle for anything less than His best for me. He wants to save me - all of us! From ourselves! Thankfully, God's goals for me are so much greater than my mere comfort and pleasure.

In the midst of the turmoil of my life, as I have begun to understand God's purposes for it, I have been learning to turn to Him and give Him my problems. In spite of the pain I have been feeling, there is relief in knowing that He is control and that He would use all these problems for my good. To wholly trust God, I must accept whatever He allows in my life.

Lately, I find myself frequently saying to God, "*I hate this; it hurts so much; but I'm going to let You worry about it, because all my efforts have failed and it's just too big for me.*" I guess this is what they call surrender. After a lifetime of trying to save myself (and my marriage, my family, etc, etc, etc), I have no steam left. So I stopped my desperate attempts to find a way out and started concentrating on just getting through one day at a time. When I put my awareness on God instead of my circumstances, I experience such relief.

I am seeing these verses in James with new eyes. They have come alive for me as never before, and, while I may not enjoy it, I am beginning to genuinely appreciate the pure joy of my pain.

May 10, Being a Sponge

"When we are reviled, we bless;
when we are persecuted, we endure;
when we are slandered, we try to conciliate;
we have become the scum of the world."
- 2 Corinthians 4:12-13

I have figured out by now that I do not have the resources within myself to overcome all my problems and live the abundant life for which I long. I need help! I am ready to allow my conditions to lead me into the presence of God and to find relief in Him. All my efforts at attaining what I want in my life have been unsuccessful. Only God can actualize it. All that is left for me is acceptance and surrender. Even as I acknowledge these truths, I understand that I cannot do anything about them. I am not supposed to, if I get the point. That is definitely the hardest part, because, as I have said before, I am a "doer". Nonetheless, God is patiently breaking down my resistance. No small task for a stubborn, strong-willed person like me.

Surrendering to God can be scary. It requires trust. What if God asks me to allow others to take advantage of me? What if God wants me to give and get nothing in return? What if He calls me to absorb the unloving behavior of others rather than responding in kind - like a human sponge?

Well, I cannot say that I have been a sponge. I can see what a difference it would make in my life and in my relationships if I were. I can see the beauty of being a sponge. Most people look down on others who show this kind of humility. We see this as a sign of weakness, rather than strength. As I think about it, though, it takes much greater strength to *"turn the other cheek"* (Luke 6:29) than it does to lash back. So what am I really losing? My pride? My selfishness? My vengeance? My bitterness? And what am I gaining? Integrity? Humility? Patience?

There is no reason for me to fear surrender to God. Who knows better than God? Certainly not me. So I want what He wants for me, no matter how hard my self will wants to fight against it. Once again, this too is God's project to complete

May 20, The Strength of Weakness

I was taking a walk, enjoying the warm spring sunshine and the opportunity to be alone with my thoughts. I began reviewing the revelations that God has recently given me about my marriage. I thought about my desire to accept it for what it is and let go of my expectations, as well as my disappointments. It was a good day; I was feeling strong and upbeat. How easy it is for me to think this way on days like this. I can do it, I thought. I can just love and accept my husband, be a sponge and trust my needs to God. Today. But what about on my bad days? What about when PMS strikes? Dismay threatened to overwhelm me as I realized how quickly my resolve would fall apart during *that* time of the month. *Who am I kidding?* All my lofty aspirations mean absolutely nothing when my hormones start raging or my body is tired and miserable.

That is when it struck me how ludicrous was my line of thinking. How many times must I go back to this same point? *In my weakness, HE is strong.* Of course, the **best** time for God to accomplish this work in my heart and in my marriage is when I am weak. I do not have to fear PMS and its destructive power. It will not inhibit God at all. In fact, I am

THE GIFT OF A BROKEN HEART

more likely to get out of God's way, because that is when I **know** that I cannot do it and must lean entirely on God's power. What a relief!

June 3, A Vacation From My Problems

"The spirit is willing, but the flesh is weak."
-Matthew 26:41

Here I am in Texas at last! Taking a vacation from my problems. I have been waiting for months for this much-needed escape. There is just one flaw in this solution, however. I can get away from my marriage, my family, the never-ending demands of my home, the thankless, mundane routine of my life, but there is one thing I cannot escape - me. I seem to follow me wherever I go! And no matter what the environment, I still have to deal with my impatience, selfishness, pride and, of course, my dear old friend PMS. I have a suspicion, though, that this is exactly the point of this trip. Once all the usual circumstances of my life are removed, I have plenty of opportunity to face myself. Clearly, God has more humbling in store for me and He is not finished showing me just how very much I need Him. My flesh is inadequate and often just plain ugly, in the best of conditions. No matter where I am or with whom, I must hold on to God for every step I take.

June 4, A Broken Leg

"He calls his own sheep by name and leads them out.
When He has brought out all his own, He goes on ahead of them,
and His sheep follow him because they know His voice."
- John 10:3-4

I woke up early this beautiful Texas morning and went outside to spend some quiet time alone with the Lord. I tried just being silent before God without attempting to fill the time with words, but my mind was distracted with so many things. I tried reading since God so often speaks to me this way and I just wanted to listen.

I read Jesus' illustrations of the shepherd and his sheep. Traditionally, if a sheep were to break its leg, the shepherd would keep it close, carrying it on his shoulders and hand feeding it. During this time of dependence, the sheep will learn to listen to the shepherd and know his voice. While considering this extreme devotion, I began to sob at the recognition *that I am that sheep.* In my brokenness, God is carrying me in order to teach me to hear and obey His voice. The thought of this great compassion overwhelmed me, and I actually found myself thanking God for the pain in my life.

I am just one of His many lost sheep in this world, and yet He cares enough to take the time to pursue me. I am in awe because I believe that I am not worthy of that kind of love. Yet, I understand that this is irrelevant. I am loved so intimately and tenderly by the God of the Universe, not because I am amazing and wonderful, but because He is.

Chapter 9

The Narrow Road

June 5, Seek and You Will Find

"Seek and you will find.
Knock and the door will be opened to you..."
- Matthew 7:7

As I have mentioned before, I went through a long dark tunnel for eight years, during which time I questioned everything I believed and searched for truth. After years of faithful Bible study, I found myself frustrated with the Bible. It seemed to be full of contradictions and I was unable to bring myself to read it for several years. I refused to read it because *I should* if I was getting nothing from it. I needed to believe in a God who is big enough to handle my doubts and speak to me through them. God seemed so silent during those years, but I continued to seek.

In the end, I decided that, while I may believe what I believe because of the environment in which I was raised, the bottom line is that I believe what I believe. Years of seeking truth did not alter that. I could not have confidence in a God who would allow any sincere seeker of truth to be led astray, so I have to assume that He is keeping me on the path that is right for me.

Many people are threatened by any beliefs that differ from their own, which is why we have so many different denominations. I, however, have come to the conclusion that I do not need anyone but God to validate my faith and I do not need to worry about judging anyone else's. I am not accountable to God for anyone but myself. I cannot presume to know what is right for anyone else. God's way of reaching each of us with His love is as unique and individual as we each are. God calls me to be His Light in this world, but it is His job to save, not mine.

Eventually, I began to emerge from my tunnel, and that is when this story began. Suddenly, I began to have an unquenchable thirst for God's Word. Verses came to life for me and took on a meaning I had never before comprehended. God seemed to be speaking to me in very powerful and direct ways through the Bible. What had before seemed like contradictions now made sense. I found answers to questions I had wrestled with for years. That started about a year and a half ago and it has not changed.

When I was younger, I read the Bible as my Christian duty. There were definitely times God spoke to me through it and I found many verses that were dear to me. Yet, it did not always bring the encouragement and inspiration to me that it does every time I read it now.

Reading the Bible is an obligation for many, with an emphasis on conquering as much as possible, while often getting absolutely nothing from it. It can be merely a way to feel worthy; another thing to check off the list of things we are *required* to do. I refuse ever to read the Bible again because I *should*. I read it when I want to, only because I want to, and, as a result, I often find that I want to. Funny how that works, isn't it? Nothing can make you *not* want to do something like thinking that you must.

My priority is quality, not quantity. Whether I read one verse or a hundred verses, I read it simply to hear what God has to say to me. God may speak to me every day through the same single verse and that might be all I need. Then there are times I cannot put it down. Either way, God's Word has become my sustenance, full of all the wisdom I need for whatever I am going through. I have always heard that the Bible is God's love letter to us, but it was not until I began personally experiencing God's love for me that I was able to hear it calling to my heart.

June 7, Missing Out On God

Therefore, there is now no condemnation for those who are in Christ Jesus,"
- Romans 8:1

I was thinking today about the idea that we are *missing out* when there is no chance for reading scripture or having a specific time set aside to spend with God. While I make that a priority in my life because I treasure that time, I do not believe that I have to confine God to a time and a place. My quiet place is within and God walks beside me wherever I go, every moment. *"Praying without ceasing"* (2 Thessalonians 5:17) just means to me that I am in constant fellowship with God in my spirit. It does not mean that I always have to talk to Him or He has to talk to me. Just like an old married couple or close friends, much of the relationship is just the comfort of being near each other as we go about our business.

As with everything else, we are taught to follow a formula and think we are wrong when we just live in day-by-day faith. It is a "dangerous" way to live; just relying on God and not on our formulas, which is really just putting our faith in ourselves - in our own good performance. I am finding it far more satisfying to live "dangerously".

I remember when I used to volunteer in the church nursery. Every time I had nursery duty, others would come and tell me that I missed the *"best service ever"*. I was always so disappointed because I thought I had really missed out. People so enjoyed saying this that it seemed almost *every* time I worked in the nursery was the *"best service ever"*.

I laugh now to think how silly it was to believe that I could ever miss out on what God has for me. How could that be? How big is my God? He is big enough to do whatever He wants in my life. He is big enough not to make mistakes that would cause us to miss what we need to hear, see or do at the very time we need it.

I love the opportunity to take a break from the busy-ness of life and be alone with the Lord. I trust that God knows the desires of my heart as well as understanding the demands on my time. Just as with reading the Bible, I refuse to pray because I think I *should*. I can just imagine how it would hurt my loved ones if they believed I was spending time with them out of a sense of duty; nor do I want to treat God that way. When I am able, that is great, but when I am not, it does not hinder my closeness to God one bit, because He never moves. He is mine and I am His every moment of every day.

June 8, True Freedom

"I tried keeping the rules and working my head off to please God, and it didn't work. So I quit being a 'law woman' so that I could be God's woman. Christ's life showed me how, and enabled me to do it.

*I identified myself completely with Him. Indeed, I have been
crucified with Christ. My ego is no longer central.
It is no longer important that I appear righteous before you or have
your good opinion, and I am no longer driven to impress God.
Christ lives in me. The life you see me living is not 'mine',
but is lived by faith in the Son of God, who loved me and gave
Himself for me. I am not going to go back on that."*
- Galatians 2:19-21

I began my morning by meditating on this passage in
Galatians. I went through each sentence one at a time. I
marveled at how well these verses described me. I became
increasingly full of gratitude as I expressed my thanks to God
for what He has done in my life; how He has opened my eyes
and set me free from my legalism. I can now find my identity
in Him, not my own performance.

My old self has been crucified - put to death - in Christ. I
can let God be in the driver's seat and my ego can retire to
the back seat. It does not matter anymore what others think
of me; I do not need to impress anyone, not even God.
Christ lives in me! I do not have to live the Christian life.
God will live it through me. No more need for striving,
controlling (or trying to), guilt, frustration, self-loathing,
failure. It is not about my effort. It's not about **me** at all.

What an incredible feeling to know that I do not have to
try anymore to measure up. I am acceptable to God as I am. I
cannot disappoint God because He already knows all my
weaknesses. I can just be me. Tears came to my eyes as these
realities sunk in and I felt so thankful for God's grace. *"I'm not
going to go back on that!"* Amen. My sentiments exactly!

June 10, Focus on Jesus

"I have told you these things, so that in Me you may have peace.
In this world you will have trouble. But take heart!
I have overcome the world."
- John 16:33

As I sat alone to pray, I began to grieve deeply for my marriage. I started crying and could not stop. Finally, I was able to calm down enough to read. God has so often spoken to me through the books that show up in my life and I was longing to find some encouragement (and hope) as I read today. Feeling desperate for comfort, I just wanted to crawl in God's lap and be held.

The point of the message I read was clear and simple. Jesus must be my center; nothing else (not even my marriage) should share His place in my life. There is no need that Jesus' presence will not meet. Nothing. I guess that is all I really need to remember. I must stop fretting over my marriage and keep my mind on Christ. I just hope that God will show me what exactly that means.

I looked up John 16:33 and meditated on it. He will never abandon me. My Father is with me. I need not allow the state of my life and relationships to shake me up. I can be assured and deeply at peace simply because He loves me. The problems will always be here, but I can take heart because Jesus has overcome the world! On this hope I stand.

June 12, What's My Hurry?

Most of us are usually in a hurry. Yet Jesus, who had more concerns pressed upon Him than perhaps anyone who ever lived, never seemed to be in a great rush. He did not stress out about all the things He had to do or worry about how He would ever get it all done. He just calmly did what He needed to do when He needed to do it. He understood how to live in the moment. He did not only talk about peace. He lived it.

God seems to put many obstacles in my way to teach me this lesson - that there is no need to rush and stress through my life because He has it all in His control. And in my hurry, there is so much I can miss of what really matters - enjoying the moment, spontaneous fellowship, stopping to "smell the roses".

Even though I am on vacation and have nowhere I have to be and nothing I have to do, I still find it difficult to slow down. Going through my days at the easy-going pace of my friend Caren has been no small challenge. Let me tell you, she has got this down. She is in no hurry - ever. The opposite of me. With her large family, it is certainly not because she has nothing to do. It would not surprise me if this is an intentional part of God's plan for me on this trip, and that He is working through Caren to produce this relaxed mentality in me as well. What is my hurry, anyway? I may never be as laid-back as Caren, but I am learning to rest in the Lord and take each moment as it comes without looking ahead and worrying about the next.

June 13, Bitterness

Growing up, I saw first-hand the effects bitterness can have on a person and, from an early age, vowed that I would never allow it to take root in my heart. I have always made a conscious effort at forgiveness. Yet, I recently recognized that I have expected from my family what their sinful nature cannot produce. I have allowed bitterness to set in when they do not live up to my expectations and I can see that this only reveals my own spiritual immaturity.

When I feel let down and frustrated in people, it is tempting to reject them and try to find others who can be counted on. The truth, though, is that I will find just as many weaknesses in the next person (and likely the same ones). If I am living in Christ and experiencing His victory, I need to see them through to the end, which means lots of love, compassion, and especially forgiveness. That is abiding in Christ. That is true Christianity; offering to others the grace that God has offered to my own sinful heart. Not my judgment, my rules or my rejection.

By loving my husband and children, God can work through me to bring healing and transformation in them. I do not believe it is the job of a Christian to emulate Jesus. I have been aware of this for myself and yet have expected it from my family. What I really want, though - for them and for me - is to share in Christ's victory over bitterness, unforgiveness, selfishness and the weakness of giving up on those we love.

As I prayed for God to produce this fruit in me, I felt a strong conviction to pass on to my family this great love that has lately become real to me in a way I have never before known. Though my love falls far short, this treasure, worth its weight in gold, is what I really wish to give to them.

Chapter 10

New Life

June 15, No Place Like Home

Home sweet home. It's good to be back. Spending time with my friends and their families has made me feel like Goldilocks - *"this porridge is too hot, this porridge is too cold; this porridge is just right."* This is where I belong and it is just right for me. While I enjoyed getting to know my friends' children and they are all wonderful, none can take the place of my own in my heart. Spending time with young children again brought back sweet memories of those days when life with my family was simple and innocent. It also gave me a glimpse of how much fun it will be to be a grandmother one day. It made me miss my own children and appreciate the great family I have.

I love my family. I love the way all my kids hang out on our bed and talk with us. I love how comfortable we are with each other. I love the honesty and trust we share. I love that, even though we cannot get through a family game night without arguing, we keep trying because we really do want to be together. I love the way my oldest daughter shares her heart with me and considers me a best friend. I love when my second daughter follows me around just to be with me and pitches in with whatever I am doing. I love how my third daughter is not afraid to show me affection in public. I love the way my youngest daughter makes me laugh and that she paints her nails a different color every day. I love getting big bear hugs from my son and the way he is always asking questions that arise from his unquenchable hunger to learn. I love that my husband is such a hard worker and can fix just about anything. I love his incredible talent for building and woodworking. I especially love that he still thinks I am beautiful after twenty-four years of marriage. I love that, even though we sometimes may not like each other, our family will always love each other and stick together through thick and thin. I love knowing that there are at least six people in this world who will be there for me no matter what. I love that my family is not *"too hard, not too soft, but just right"* for me.

I'm with Dorothy. There *is* no place like home.

June 18, From My Head to My Heart

I have been re-reading a book called "*Sidetracked in the Wilderness*" by Michael Wells. There is a test in it to discern how you **feel** (not what you **"know"**) about God in your worst moments. I took the test about a year ago and was amazed at how completely different my answers are today.

Here are some of my favorites:

<u>*A Year Ago*</u>	**TODAY**
When I think about being with God, I feel...	
Hopeless, discouraged	**HAPPY**

When I need to trust God, I feel...

Afraid   **CONFIDENT**

Sometimes I feel angry with God when...

He seems so silent   **I DON'T GET**
and distant   **ANGRY WITH**
                               GOD ANYMORE

Something I would change about myself to please God is (this one is HUGE and the reason my answer changed is NOT because I think I have it all together now but because I feel loved and accepted as I am)...

Everything   **NOTHING**

When I think of God's commands, I feel...

Overwhelmed   **FREE**

I can really rely on God when...

I don't know   **ALWAYS**

In my relationship with God, I am always sure He will...

Not sure of   **WORK ALL**
anything   **THINGS FOR MY**
                               GOOD

The thing that frightens me most about God is...

I will never be able   **NOT A THING**
to please Him

Most Christians know the answers that we are "supposed" to give to questions like these, but the point is to answer honestly - just between you and God. I was completely candid both times. As I compare my answers, I am amazed at the transformation God has worked in my heart over these past 15 months.

For most of my life, I have struggled with as much doubt and guilt as anyone, even while trying desperately to follow and please this God that I did not trust. I was in the miserable Christian trap that we pretend does not exist. No one could have convinced me that I was on the wrong path in pursuit of my faith. I was on the same path as every other sincere Christian I knew - the path I had been taught to follow from the time I was a child. Then God broke through to me...finally, finally, finally. He took the blinders from my eyes and let me see the kind of Father He truly is. And now, I believe. I thought I always did, but I did not. Now I really do believe in God. I am no longer afraid to place my life into His Hands.

I wish I could give to everyone this gift that God has given to me. Yet I know better. It is a journey we each must take. It is something only God can do - getting what we "know" from our heads into our hearts. If He can do it for this doubting soul, then He can do it for anyone.

June 19, Being in the Minority

I have always been different. A salmon swimming upstream. It's not that I like being an oddball; it's just that I am determined to follow my convictions rather than follow the crowd. Inevitably, that leaves me doing weird stuff like homebirths, homeschooling, unconventional eating habits, and abandoning organized religion.

Being a follower of Christ in itself puts me in the minority. I do not mind much because I do not get my sense of worth from fitting in. Yet, I can see that being in the minority does not mean that I should isolate myself from those who are different from me, hiding from the world and only associating with those who share my beliefs.

That is what the majority does, but that is not what Jesus did. He hung out with the tax collectors and prostitutes rather than the respected members of society. He was not afraid to reach out to the hurting world and share their burdens.

The majority concentrate on big accomplishments; the minority on being faithful in small things. Mainstream religious thinking encourages following formulas for a quick solution to problems, rather than teaching a moment-by-moment dependence on Christ. It seems more popular to value knowledge and the law than to value love and grace. Most are busy *doing*, while only a few seem to discover the freedom in just *being*. The majority of people believe that some are more worthy than others. A minority believe that we all fall short, and yet we are all worthy of love. The mass follow a teaching; a smaller number follow the Teacher.

There was a time where I was more part of the majority, but thanks to the grace of God in my life, I am increasingly becoming part of the minority. I am so grateful for that. Once again, I am marching to a different beat, but I am glad to be in some excellent company.

June 27, My Mound of Dirt

"So we're not giving up. How could we?
Even though on the outside it often looks like things are falling apart on us,
on the inside, where God is making new life,
not a day goes by without His unfolding grace."
- 2 Corinthians 4:16

It is becoming increasingly obvious to me that my marriage is under attack. Even my discouragement about it is from my adversary, who wants me to give up. I trust that he cannot defeat me because he is himself defeated. I have already surrendered my marriage to God. I had to surrender it again.

I read an illustration of how the pit the enemy digs for us only creates a mound of dirt that brings us up to the presence of God. I love that. Therefore, I do not need to be afraid of the pit. God can use every obstacle in my life to draw me to Him. Hope for my marriage returned. I need not worry about what will happen to us tomorrow. God has it under control, and thankfully, I do not have to.

July 16, God is Great, God is Good

Sometimes I think my journal is so redundant. And yet, this journey for me has indeed been about repeating the same few lessons over and over. Each time God gets His truth through to me on a little bit deeper level. For most of us, I suppose, it seems to take constant repetition to get through to our stubborn hearts and minds. All I have to do is think about raising my children to see the reality of this. I have spent years repeating myself to them in an effort to teach them the most basic ideas. And my kids are very smart and intuitive. It's just human nature.

It occurred to me the other day that the lesson of my life boils down to one very simple truth: God is good. Period. If I genuinely believe in God's goodness, then I can trust Him. If I completely trust God, then I feel safe in His care and rest in the knowledge that He is indeed in control. I can walk in childlike faith without worry, believing that my Daddy will take care of me no matter what happens. I will effortlessly experience the serenity that we all spend our entire existence seeking. So, in actuality, if anyone wanted to know what God is doing in my life, all they would need to do is read this one journal entry and they would know. That is all there is to it - God is good. I say this like it is not taking me a lifetime to learn.

July 17, Three Simple Steps

"For it is by grace you have been saved, through faith,
and this is not from yourselves, it is the gift of God--
not by works, so that no one can boast.
For we are God's handiwork, created in Christ Jesus to do good works,

which God prepared in advance for us to do."
- Ephesians 2:8-10

I am reading a book about finding joy. Someone I love gave it to me, and being a loyal person, I want to share in what is meaningful to those I love. Otherwise, I am not sure I would still be reading it. At first, I was thinking that it is reminiscent of my old legalistic days. I have read many books like this, I thought. Then the author made some great points and she definitely stresses relationship with God as the answer to experiencing joy, so I have tried to read with a receptive attitude. I do not find reading it to be a waste of my time; it is an encouraging reminder of how far I have come, and of course, God can speak to me through anything.

Last night, however, I got to the point where many religious books eventually seem to arrive. All I have to do is follow these easy steps and everything will fall into place in my life. I know all too well the roller coaster ride of following religious methods; the hopeful, diligent effort followed by the disappointing sense of failure and self-condemnation, none of which seemed to lead me closer to my goal of a fulfilling spiritual life as promised. The *"it's all about me"* plan; God is just waiting to give me a new life if I can just manage to get it right and follow a few simple (?) steps.

The first step is obviously the diligent study of God's Word. While I value the wisdom and truth of the Bible tremendously, I am glad that I am no longer stuck in believing that relationship with God is dependent upon my discipline. I am also actually glad that following steps and formulas did not work for me, because, in my defeat, I discovered victory over the law. When I finally gave up and quit working so hard for the abundant life, it found me. God is able. I am not. It's ok. It makes life so much easier; it really has lowered my stress level considerably. Now, instead of trying to follow three simple steps to success, I think I will just leave it to the Expert. He is more than capable.

August 6, Letting Loose

> *"There is a time for everything,*
> *and a season for every activity under the heavens...*
> *a time to weep and a time to laugh,*
> *a time to mourn and a time to dance."*
>
> - Ecclesiastes 3:1, 4

Someone recently asked me what I do for fun. When pressed, I had to admit that I could go on forever telling myself that I will make time for fun when I have more time. When will that be? I took the point to heart. Life is short and there is more to it than doing my duty. I have the responsibility part down; I need to learn to take time to enjoy it too. Fun is not so much a thing you do as an attitude you have. So forget the plans for tomorrow, which may never come. The fun should start today. All I had to do was look for my moment. It came quicker than I expected.

Going home from an appointment in the city, I took the train to the station where I had parked my car. It was the middle of a workday and very few people were onboard. After several stops, I looked around and realized that I was the only one in my car. *I am all by myself here,* I thought. How rare is that? I suddenly felt a great sense of freedom. I could do anything I wanted and no one would know. I could jump up and down, scream, run around, anything. Of course, I am a dignified adult so I would not do anything like that. Would I? I began eyeing the poles. I was listening to music on my IPod and thinking how fun it would be to dance. I could dance around those poles. No, that would be crazy, silly. What if someone saw me? So what if they did? Then I decided this was a once in a lifetime opportunity that I just could not let pass by. What the hell, I thought, as I jumped up from my seat and began to dance and swing around those poles. Weeee! WooHoo! I actually yelled at the top of my lungs. *Now this is fun!* I even swung from the ceiling poles like a kid on the monkey bars, touching them with my feet.

By the time the train arrived at my stop, I was feeling as free and light as a bird. There is something very liberating about stepping outside the confines of society and letting loose. When the door opened, I was grinning from ear to ear, very amused by my little secret. *If only you knew what I was just doing,* I thought at the passersby. I caught people looking at me, puzzled by my huge smile. I imagined they were wondering what I found so funny or if maybe I was just plain nuts. Maybe they would be right. Some even smiled back, my glee contagious. I practically skipped all the way to my car. I had a wonderful drive home. *Thank you, Lord,* I reflected, *for reminding me how to be a kid again and take pleasure in the simplest things in life.* I think Jesus was really onto something when He said we need to receive the Kingdom of Heaven like a little child. How very much we miss when we grow up and lose our innocent pleasure at the wonder of life.

August 9, My Path and My Purpose

What are my path and my purpose in life? This is the question of the year for me, and one I spend much time pondering. Twenty-one years ago, I had a very clear vision of my path and purpose. As I began to have children, I felt a strong calling to be a full-time mother. I still can think of no greater calling, even as I look back with mixed emotions about the success of my first mission in life. The Bible says that you do not reap in the same season that you sow. Therefore, it is probably premature to come to any conclusions yet, even though it is a great temptation to me. Of one thing I am confident; I have given it my all. I concluded some time back that I would no longer berate myself for my failings. I have devoted myself to my family and loved them to the best of my ability, and I continue to do so. I do not know what more I could expect of myself and I do not think God expects any more than that either.

Uncertainty about my past achievements has left me somewhat tentative about moving forward with new goals for this next season of my life. Stepping outside my comfort zone and starting on a new, unknown path is intimidating, whatever it may entail. What if I am rejected? What if people do not appreciate what I have to give? I have enough experience with the sting of rejection and criticism to make me hesitant. What if my best is not good enough again? What if I fail?

There is always risk in life no matter what path we take. There is always failure. I *will* fail sometimes as I have many times before, and through it, I have learned some of the most valuable lessons. Therefore, even though it still frightens me a little, I do not want to live in fear or miss opportunities because of it. It is tempting to project into the future and allow the possibilities to intimidate me, but I cannot see the future. I can only take one-step at a time, knowing that God will direct my path and lead me to my next purpose. There is no rush. Baby steps. I can do that.

Chapter 11

Falling

September 22, Invisible

> *"But when you do your giving,*
> *do not let your left hand know*
> *what your right hand is doing,*
> *so that your gift may be in secret.*
> *And your Father, who sees in secret,*
> *will reward you."*
> - Matthew 6:3-4

I have been feeling resentful lately. I know I am only hurting myself by wallowing in these feelings, but it has been a constant battle for me. Now that my homeschooling career is over, I expected to have so much time to do the things I have long waited to do. The truth is, however, that running a home takes up as much time as you have. If you have all day, it can take all day, especially if you want to do it well. And I always want to do things well. These days, however, I yearn for more. I want a chance to pursue my dreams as well; dreams I have put on hold for so many years. So, I found myself once again resenting my family, their expectations, and their ungrateful attitudes toward me.

Last week, as my frustration grew with my inability to get beyond the thankless chores, I finally acknowledged that my goals are not going to come to me. I have to make them a priority. I decided to take the time to do some things that are important to me. I signed up for an art class, wrote a couple of long overdue journal entries, took a meal to a neighbor, and went to a water aerobics class. I felt much better.

I do not always receive appreciation for the things I do, and sometimes it makes me feel invisible. Still, I am not invisible to God. He reminds me that He notices every sacrifice I make and every disappointment I experience. My efforts are not in vain, but God is using them to build something beautiful. True, I might not see it completed in my lifetime, but it will last an eternity.

It is ok that they do not see, that they do not appreciate. In truth, if I am doing it right, they will never see. Being invisible is actually a gift that can set me free from pride and selfishness. My work is for God; my sacrifices are for Him. What really matters is that God sees. That is all the recognition I need.

September 26, Worthless or Priceless?

I am reading a wonderful book about one man's journey out of religion into finding God called *"Divine Nobodies"* by Jim Palmer. In it, he tells of a beautiful illustration of a young, handicapped girl in a wheelchair with her father kneeling next to her reading a book that is resting in her lap. He has his arm around her, and she is slumped over against his shoulder, with her head resting against the side of his face. She cannot walk, talk or even sit up straight; she is just sitting there unresponsive as her dad animatedly reads to her.

I was deeply moved by this illustration and the author's response to it. As he explained, this little girl has absolutely nothing to offer her father. She cannot reciprocate his love in any way. Yet, his adoration for her is apparent. She may be useless to the world, but, to her father, she is priceless.

In this world, we are valued for what we have to give. Even in the church, the emphasis is often on what we can do for God. We work so hard trying to get God to like us. Would God still love me if I had nothing to offer Him? If I could do utterly nothing but receive

His love, would God see me as His treasure?

I know how very much I love my own children and that nothing they do could diminish that love. They do not have to *do* anything to earn my love; they just have it.

I am reminded of Jesus' comment that,

"If you then, who are evil, know how to give good gifts to your children, how much more will your Father in Heaven give good gifts?" (Matthew 7:11).

If I am able to love my children so much, how much greater must be God's love for His children?

It is hard for me to begin to grasp being loved so profoundly. Yet, it is slowly becoming real for me and I find myself in awe that such a magnificent God could find such value in an insignificant little human like me, who really has nothing to offer Him. It is so unlike human love that I may need reminding again tomorrow, but for today, I am just going to lean against His face and soak up all that adoration.

One year later...
August 18, Total Commitment

I have spent the past two months spiraling down into a bleak abyss. It all began when I came home from our anniversary vacation with my hopes high regarding my husband's renewed promises of total commitment to our relationship. It did not take long before I began believing that they were empty promises.

Falling back into the routine of caring for my family, and feeling taken for granted, I fell further and further into depression. I could not bring myself to reach out to any of my friends, and as time passed, I found that no one was concerned with where I had gone. I was not missed. That only sent me into deeper despair as I started thinking that no one really cared.

Finally, one friend reached out to me from her own pit of despair, and I was convicted that I had not been willing to get beyond my self-pity to be there for her. As we resumed our weekly phone conversations, she became my lifeline to sanity. I found comfort in knowing I was not alone.

During one of our conversations, my friend suggested that I search for the underlying cause of my frustrations, with my marriage in particular. I asked God to show me if there was something I was missing. He must have answered that prayer because it was not long before the source began to become clear to me. The first thought that came to mind was that I do not feel valued by anyone. When I experienced the deep pain of that thought, which brings an aching in my heart every time, I knew that I had touched on a very raw nerve.

I have done a good deal of soul searching in the days since then, seeking the root of my pain. I could sum it up with one word - rejection. I thought first of my own family; my husband and children. I suppose I have always had the subconscious assumption that if I was totally committed to them, gave them my all, and loved them completely, this would be reciprocated. Of course, they all love me, but I have faced more rejection from these most important people in my life than everyone else I have ever known put together. I often feel my family tolerates me while they do not really like me. I rarely experience the feeling of being valued by any of them. They want me to take care of them, but do not see me as a person with needs and feelings. They are annoyed when I allow evidence of these needs and feelings to show. I understand this is normal with children, at least; I probably did not consider my mother's needs or feelings much either, and I did not even always like her. My husband is another matter, however, and I am sure his lack of support has exacerbated my feelings.

Wanting to really get to the heart of the matter, I pushed myself to consider if there is a deeper reason that I am so wounded by my family's rejections. I went further back and revisited some of the wounds of rejection I experienced as a child from some members of my family. As I looked back on my life, I recognized this repeated pattern of rejection. In the 13 years that we have lived here, my family and I have never been fully accepted in this non-transient community where most people have grown up together. We have yet to find any place where we belong.

Since rejection has become a way of life for me and because they are my children, I take personally the many rejections my children have had to face. It must be that no one likes them because they are part of me. The fact that my husband is impervious to it all only makes it more personal and lonely for me. I have no doubt that I long ago learned to expect rejection and probably even see it where it does not truly exist. Perhaps I subconsciously even draw it. That does not make it hurt one bit less.

As pathetic as it sounds, this is the honest condition of my inner being at this point. In the midst of these painful revelations, God has reminded me that He is the only One that I need; the only One on whom I should depend. The only One that will never leave me nor forsake me. No one else is able to give me the love I need. The problem is that I do not know how to stop needing others to love and accept me. I cannot heal my own wounded heart or change myself into a selfless servant. I cannot physically see, hear or feel God. I have no clue how to find all my satisfaction in a relationship with God.

Amazingly, in spite of all God has revealed to me in these past two years, right now I am unsure how to fully trust and rest in God. I also certainly do not know how to let God fill the emptiness in me. If I did, I sure as heck would not be holding my "cup" up to other people to fill. He is all I ever wanted, but for some reason, it feels lately like He evades me. I wish I understood what God wants from me. I wish I could always rejoice in His love for me and be free from discouragement. I suppose it is good to understand all of this, but it does not really help me unless God chooses to deliver me. The only thing I have left is hope. I am trying to hold on to it, but to be honest, it's slipping.

Another year later...
July 10, Overwhelming Grief

> *"I am overcome by sorrow; strengthen me,*
> *as You have promised.*
> *Keep me from going the wrong way,*
> *and in your goodness teach me your law.*
> *I have chosen to be obedient;*
> *I have paid attention to Your judgments.*
> *I have followed your instructions,*
> *Lord; don't let me be put to shame."*
> - Psalms 119:28-31

It has been almost a year since I have written anything. It has been a very stressful and hectic year. After a twenty-three year career as a stay-at-home mom, I rejoined the work force, taking a full time (plus) job. While I have enjoyed being a working woman again, more than that I have appreciated the escape from my home life. I have become increasingly discouraged about my marriage and all my attempts to restore it have failed. I think we have both practically given up and are just going through the motions. What does a loyal woman do who has made a commitment of *"until death do us part"*, yet feels her soul dying from the effort of keeping it?

To make matters worse, recently I lost my grandfather - a man I have felt closer to than any other. He has always been one of my greatest supporters. His unfailing love gave me a glimpse of my Heavenly Father's. I knew I would never be truly alone in this world as long as my grandaddy was around. Now he is gone. The hole his absence has created in my life is cavernous.

I have endeavored to hold on to the truths God has taught me in these past few years, leaning on Him for my strength. I know God loves me and He is with me, but I have never felt so alone. I put my hope in His faithfulness and His promises, but I am growing weak and weary from heartache.

August 26, Bittersweet Relief

I left my husband. According to him, I abandoned our family, even though I am only five miles away and spend time with the kids every day. According to me, it was a matter of survival. Mine, at least. I understood that he would never leave our home, so the only way I could get this much needed separation was if I myself left. I did not ask for a divorce. As I tried to explain to him, I believe we just need some time apart. I am not ready to give up on our marriage just yet. Maybe I should. I have certainly given it enough years and enough effort. Yet I am still hoping and praying that we can break the unhealthy patterns and find a way to make a fresh start. I suppose I am hoping for a miracle.

The weight of our dying marriage was slowly crushing me and I knew that desperate measures were needed if I was to keep my hope alive. I felt alone in a house full of people. If it is actually possible to starve to death for lack of love, I was well on my way.

As I prayed for God to rescue me, His answer seemed to come in a phone call from an acquaintance I had not spoken with in a couple of years. She offered me a place to stay with her and her children while I sort things out. It did not take long to decide. I knew I could not go on this way for much longer. I feel sad, but I also feel great relief. Every day I am away, I can feel the tension melting just a little bit more.

My husband's response to my departure has been to meet with a lawyer and begin divorce proceedings. I left him and, in his mind, that is the end. Even though I am the one that left, his decision is breaking my heart. My children are also alienating me and it seems I am losing not only my marriage but also the family into which I have invested my entire life. It is bittersweet - this sensation of finally being able to breathe again mingled with heart wrenching loss of all that I love. *God help me. I need a miracle.*

September 15, Storm on the Horizon

I've come to start a fire on this earth...
I've come to change everything,
turn everything right side up—
how I long for it to be finished!
Do you think I have come to bring peace to the earth?
No, I have come to divide people against each other!
From now on families will be split apart, three in favor of me,
and two against--or two in favor and three against.
'Father will be divided against son and son against father;
mother against daughter and daughter against mother...
Then He turned to the crowd and said:
'When you see clouds coming in from the west, you say,
Storm's coming—and you're right.' "
- Luke 12:49-54

I came upon these words in Luke spoken by Jesus and thought, *"This is exactly what is happening to my family!"* It is a disturbing message and yet I know that those who choose to follow Christ are despised by many in this world, just as Jesus Himself was. Often the rejection can even come from your own family.

There was a time when I believed that my husband and I shared the same faith, but it seems we have chosen different paths. The result has been this devastating division in our home. I try to take heart in the knowledge that God is in control, but how can I be at peace with the destruction of my family? I see the storm coming and there is nothing I can do to stop it. Nothing but pray.

This helplessness to save my family is breaking my heart. If I thought I felt rejected in my home before, it could not compare to this feeling now of being essentially cast out of my own family. I am unwanted by the loved ones around whom I have centered my whole life. I have never felt more isolated than I do right now. I am like a tiny ship floating alone in a vast ocean, painfully aware of just how easily I could capsize from the first big wave that comes along.

Thankfully, I do have an anchor in the One who has promised never to leave me. I am clinging to that Anchor.

September 18, Deliver Me From Temptation

Even as I am feeling a desperate need for love, I am withdrawing from everyone. Usually I am the one who takes care of everyone else, but I cannot be there for anyone now. The anguish in my soul is too great even to talk about it. I know God loves me, but I would give anything just to be held. Unfortunately, at this point, there is no one to hold me. Recognizing my vulnerability, I understand that I must choose my steps carefully, so I pray for strength and wisdom.

Every morning, after I pick up my younger children at the house and drop them off at school, I find a quiet spot to stop and pray before heading to work. My prayers are grave and distressed these days.

Lord, please save my marriage. Save my family. I don't know how.
Take these burdens for me. They are far too heavy.
I feel so discarded and unloved. So exposed and raw.
Please do not allow any man to come into my life to tempt me.
I am longing for love and I know I am not strong enough to
resist that kind of attention right now. Please, Lord, keep me from
more temptation than I can bear. Help me to do the right thing.
My life is in Your Hands. Give me strength to hold on.

September 29, Strong Women Don't Quit

Lately, I cannot seem to eat or sleep at all. I have lost over 20 lbs in the past couple of weeks. If I manage to get two hours of sleep a night, I am doing well. My body is like a car constantly stuck in high RPM. My nerves are raw; my heart seems to be endlessly racing. I have gotten into the habit of coming home from my 10-12 hour workdays and trying to calm myself down with a couple of glasses of wine. I hoped it would help me sleep. It doesn't, but at least it does enable me to relax a little.

I finally went to the doctor in an effort to discover why my body is acting so crazy. She found nothing wrong and gave me some sleeping pills (which did nothing to help me sleep). She says I am fine. Then, I must be fine. So I keep going. Living on almost no sleep and an alcohol diet fueling my long workdays. It's ok, though, because I am a strong woman. Strong women keep going when the going gets tough. I have overcome many obstacles and hardships in my life. I will get through this. But...*Where are you, God? Why don't You save my family?*

October 9, Point of No Return

My friend has a teenage son living here in the home where I am staying. At first, I thought he was just a troublemaker. He has apparently gotten into drugs and frequently been in and out of juvy. His mother is convinced that he has been entertaining young ladies at the house while she is at work and she is afraid he will get one of them pregnant.

He seems to have many problems. Yet I have discovered that he is tender-hearted and insightful. Having experienced turbulent teenage years myself, I can relate to his struggle. That season of life can be the most difficult for us sensitive souls, especially the male ones.

My heart goes out to him and I have endeavored to encourage him toward a more positive path for his life. As I have gotten to know him, I have found that I enjoy his company and appreciate his deep introspective nature.

Since we both have been suffering from insomnia, we often find ourselves up talking and playing cards late into the night after every else has gone to bed. An unusual and unlikely friendship has slowly been developing between us.

As our bond has been growing stronger, my feelings for him

begin to change. With a maturity far beyond his years, I find myself able to relate to him as I could someone my own age. Somewhere along the way, I have stopped seeing him as a kid and am beginning to experience a very strong attraction to this special, unique young man.

I realize that alcohol and sleep deprivation may be clouding my judgment and I am wrestling with my feelings. I seem to be losing the battle as, incredibly, I find myself falling in love. Or maybe losing my mind. I have been on my guard with men; wary and careful. I never dreamed I would need to guard myself against feelings for one this young. Through my long sleepless nights, I pour out my fears to God.

God, help me! Save me!
How could I be in love someone so much younger than me? A teenager!!
This is crazy! This is sick. What is wrong with me?
I don't understand how I can feel this way! HELP!

October 23, The Choice

My husband has had a change of heart. He tells me that God convicted him of the way he has treated me and he asked my forgiveness. He wants to try to win me back but it is too late for me. I am in love, yet not with him. I did not admit this, though I did tell him that I no longer feel anything for him. I do want our marriage restored and our family reunited, so I agreed to remain open. He has begun to court me and try to work on all the things I have tried to get him to see for years. Why couldn't this have happened a month ago?

Somewhere along the way, I stopped looking to God to meet my needs and decided to take care of myself. Through my alcohol haze, I have justified my choices. I have been avoiding God. I did not want to be convicted. I just wanted to be happy. Now all I feel is guilt. With my husband now making the effort to reconcile, I know I cannot live with this deceit. I do want to do the right thing, but it is breaking my heart.

I am procrastinating, I know, but walking away from love back to duty is one of the hardest things I have ever had to do.

PART

TWO

Chapter 12

Job's Despair

"I was born naked. And I'll leave here naked.
You have given and You have taken away.
May Your name be praised."
- Job 1:21

January 27, Crushed

"I cannot keep from speaking. I must express my anguish.
My bitter soul must complain. My eyes are swollen with weeping,
and I am but a shadow of my former self. My days are over.
My hopes have disappeared. My heart's desires are broken.
My spirit is crushed, and my life is nearly snuffed out.
The grave is ready to receive me."
- Job 7:1, 17:1, 7, 11

It is not being in jail that is the hardest part. It is harsh and cold and cruel here, but I hardly notice. My suffering is internal and nothing can compare. My heart is beyond broken over the pain I have caused those I love. I spend much of my waking hours on my knees asking God's forgiveness and praying for those I have unintentionally hurt by my actions. Though I experience God's instantaneous forgiveness, grace and mercy, it is much more difficult to forgive myself. I am also very aware that forgiveness from people will come much slower, if ever. Even in the midst of my deep sorrow, I feel God's loving arms around me. It is the only comfort I have right now and I cling to it, though I do not feel I deserve it.

I am drawn to the book of Job in the Bible and find myself relating to Job in a way I never before could. His words express my feelings perfectly.

> *"In the grave, sinful people don't cause trouble anymore.*
> *And there those who are tired find rest.*
> *Prisoners sleep undisturbed,*
> *never again to wake up to the bark of the guards...*
> *Why does God bother giving light to the miserable,*
> *why bother keeping bitter people alive?*
> *Those who want in the worst way to die and can't,*
> *who can't imagine anything better than death,*
> *who count the day of their death the happiest day of their life?*
> *What's the point of life when it doesn't make sense,*
> *when God blocks all the roads to meaning?...*
> *God hasn't told me what will happen to me.*
> *He has surrounded me with nothing but trouble.*
> *I sigh instead of eating food. Groans pour out of me like water.*
> *What I was afraid of has come on me.*
> *What I worried about has happened to me.*
> *I don't have any peace and quiet. I can't find any rest.*
> *All I have is trouble...*
> *I'm so weak that I no longer have any hope.*
> *Things have gotten so bad that I can't wait for help anymore."*
> -Job 3:17-26, 6:11

Job's situation was different from mine, but I could have written these words myself. The grief in my heart crushes me and I long for the sweet escape of death. Yet I know this is not my choice to make. My life is in God's hands and, as desperately as I want to go Home, it is not yet my time.

January 30, Forgotten

> *"My relatives have gone away;*
> *my closest friends have forgotten me.*
> *I am loathsome to my own family.*
> *All my intimate friends detest me;*

those I love have turned against me.
Have pity on me, my friends, have pity,
for the hand of God has struck me.
A 'woman's' friends should love her when her hope is gone.
They should be faithful to her, e
ven if she stops showing respect for the Mighty One.
But my friends aren't faithful to me.
Why don't you forgive me for the wrong things I've done?"
-Job 6:14-15, 7:21, 19:14, 17, 19, 21

When Job was at his lowest, his friends judged and lectured him. I understand how he felt. I am alone in my agony. My friends and family have all abandoned me. I can understand that they are confused, disappointed in me, some angry with me.

When you hit rock bottom, this is the time you learn who really loves you, who is truly there for you. Others may judge my heart without actually knowing what is in my heart. Yet, there is only one who knows my heart, who sees the ugliness in my heart, who sees the beauty in my heart, who loves and accepts me as I am. The One, at this point, who is my only reason to live.

February 5, The Good People

"You're familiar with the command, 'Do not murder.'
I'm telling you that anyone who is so much as
angry with another is guilty of murder.
You have also heard, 'Do not commit adultery.
'But here is what I tell you.
Do not even look at a woman in the wrong way.
Anyone who does has already committed adultery with her in his heart."
- Matthew 5:21-22, 27-28

Job's friends express the Christian formula for life that is still prevalent today:

"Commit yourself to God completely.
Reach out your hands to Him for help.
Get rid of all the sin you have.

Don't let anything that is evil stay in your tent.
Then you can face others without shame.
You can stand firm without being afraid."
-Job 11:13-15

They believed Job's problems came from the sinfulness hidden in his heart and that if he would just repent and stop sinning, God would bless him and all his problems would go away.

Job's anwer to them was:

"People who have an easy life look down
on those who have problems.
They think trouble comes only to
those whose feet are slipping."
- Job 12:5

Job understood what his friends did not; that *"**all** have sinned and fallen short of the glory of God"*. It seems to be human nature to rank sins, looking down on others whose sins do not tempt us and excusing our own inclinations as minor offenses. We tend to label some people "good" and some people "bad", even if we do not say so out loud. And the sin of pride runs rampant among the "good" people. Jesus said that to God all sin is the same; no one sin greater than any other. Hate is murder as lust is adultery. Therefore, God, in His infinite wisdom and love for us, has given us this beautiful gift called grace, knowing that this is exactly what every single one of us need desperately and none of us can earn. Grace that is greater than **all** our sin.

I think many who knew me have decided that maybe they did not really know me. How could a good person fall in love with someone so young? How could a good person be put in jail? Good people do not get into trouble with the law, right? They were correct. A good person would not. I am not a good person. I have never claimed to be a good person. I am a person in dire need of God's endless grace. That is all I have ever claimed to be. That does not make me different from anyone else. I am just the same as the most upstanding, law abiding citizen. I am just the same as the most "low-life" sinner.

What is now crystal clear to me is that I can never again judge another person's acts no matter how heinous they might seem. I appreciate what only one who has done something they never believed they were capable of doing can completely understand. We truly do not know the weakness that lies dormant in our hearts until just the right combination of events come at just the right time to bring it to life.

This humbling insight into the wickedness of my own heart has taught me the meaning of grace in a way that no words ever could. I consider myself truly blessed to have learned that I am in need of it every bit as much as the most reviled of sinners (even before I unwillingly joined that "club"). For it is only in seeing our monumental need for grace that we are able to truly receive it; that we are truly free from the bondage of sin.

During this disastrous time in my life, when I most need grace, I have received it much more freely from God than from my fellow sinners, even those who have claimed to love me. As much as that hurts, I know that it is only His grace that I need. Ever merciful and kind, He reminds me that I am not the mistakes I have made. I am not my failures. I am not the sins I have committed. I am a child of the Almighty. Chosen. Forgiven. Redeemed. Dearly loved.

February 7, Letter from the Other Side

My daughter sent me a note from my mother that she found among my things and thought I might appreciate. It was written on my 20th birthday, but it could have been written today.

"Dearest Avery,

On the day you were born, I was as happy as it's possible to be and I loved you more than I can say. Today, I love you even more and <u>no</u> <u>one</u> could be prouder of a daughter. You have become a beautiful, sweet, sensitive young woman.

I know you are going thru a trying period in your life and it hurts me that you've reached a point where I cannot help you, except by giving you my love and support. That you will always have.

I pray to God every day that He will direct you to whatever you need to fulfill you and set you in the direction which will make you happy. I know that

day will come - I <u>believe in you</u> and <u>you</u> must <u>believe in yourself</u>. Look to the future, Darling! There are better things to come.
    I love you very much.
    Happy Birthday! Mom"

Chills ran through me as I read it, feeling as though my mother had reached out to me from the grave to encourage me. I do not think my mother would be so proud of me right now, but I know that she would still believe in me and still support me. A time like this is when a girl really needs her mother. She is one I am sure would not have abandoned me. Yet, as much as I miss her and as alone as I feel, I would never want my mother to have to go through this with me. As a mother myself, I can certainly understand it would be as hard for her as it is for me; maybe even harder. A loving mother deeply feels her children's pain like no one else can. In fact, one of the most unbearable aspects of my situation has been the suffering it has caused my own children. That is much more difficult to deal with than my own pain. I guess this is something they cannot understand until they have their own children.

Even though this note made me long for my mother more than ever, it was a comfort. It was so eerily relevant to the present that I sensed God's loving hand behind it. A mother's love never dies, even when she does. She has been gone for over thirteen years, but today Mom sent me a love letter. What a gift! *Thank you, Lord.*

August 8, Though He Slay me

"Though He slay me, yet will I trust in Him."
-Job 13:15

They took my journal - 175 days of it; everything I have written for the past 6 months, pouring out my deep pain on the pages. It feels like I have been raped. Apparently, I was betrayed by my closest friend in here. I am told I have no rights. Another punch in the stomach. I feel so sick. I cannot eat. The depression and hopelessness I have been trying so hard to hold back for this past year is swallowing me whole. I am so exhausted from hurting and being beat down for so long that I do not know if I can get back up this time. Not thinking; not feeling; praying is so hard - I am just empty.

August 12, Bond of Hope

"I remember how I suffered and wandered.
I remember how bitter my life was.
I remember it very well.
My spirit is very sad deep down inside me.
But here is something else I remember.
And it gives me hope. The Lord loves me very much.
So I haven't been completely destroyed.
His loving concern never fails.
His great love is new every morning.
Lord, how faithful You are!
The Lord is everything I will ever need,
so I will put my hope in Him.
The Lord is good to those who put their hope in Him.
It is good when people wait quietly for the Lord to save them."
-Lamentations 3:19-25

All I can do is lay in bed, pray and sleep. My prayers are pretty simple these days: *"Forgive me for giving up. I just can't anymore. I'm drowning, Lord. Save me!"* God's love is all I have and I beg Him to let me come Home. Yet, ironically, it is the suffering of the other women here that prevents me from giving up entirely.

A new girl got extremely sick from kidney stones and the nurse would do nothing to help her, so my compassion for her moved me to get out of bed this evening. I put a cool cloth on her head and gave her my blanket, then sat with her and prayed, feeling helpless to ease her pain. After many hours, they finally came to take her, hopefully to the hospital. God, in His wisdom, gave me a chance to take my mind off me for a while to care for someone else and it actually made me feel better.

After I returned to my bed and my despair, a friend came to check on me. She gave me a little lecture about forgiving myself and not giving up. She was tough on me and I was deeply touched by her concern, so I got up and hugged her. I convinced myself that I could push through this a little longer and trust God to carry me. I rallied a bit and even ate a little, but it was not long before I crumbled again. I ended up back in bed, crying my heart out. Once again, my friends came to cheer me with their support and encouragement. God has sent women into my life who refuse to let me quit and I am so grateful for their kindness.

There is bond that develops among people who are forced to suffer together in close quarters. While this environment can be fertile ground for cruelty, many of us quickly forget that we are strangers and offer what comfort we can to one another. A little sympathy goes a long way in this callous world. We help each other not to lose hope, because no one can survive without hope.

Chapter 13

Love Lifted Me

"I waited patiently for the Lord.
He turned to me and heard my cry.
He lifted me out of the slimy pit, out of the mud and mire.
He set my feet on a rock and gave me a firm place to stand.
He put a new song in my mouth, a hymn of praise to our God.
Many will see and fear the Lord and put their trust in Him."
- Psalm 40:1-3

"Weeping may last through the night,
but joy comes with the morning."
- Psalm 30:5

August 13, My Safe Place
"You are my place of safety.
I will be glad and full of joy because You love me.
You saw that I was hurting. You took note of my great pain.
You have put me in a safe place. I trust in You, Lord.
My life is in Your hands."
- Psalms 31:2-8

Amazing the difference a day can make. I woke up this morning with a new conviction to accept my situation and believe that God is working for my good. I fully surrendered all that I have been resisting - losing my journal, living in this loud open-dorm POD with constant drama and zero privacy, being rejected by whoever is currently mad at me, the tremendous loss of all those that I love, and the possibility of being sentenced to more jail time.

God showed me that I have been living in constant fear of the next blow - expecting it - and not really trusting in His good will for me. God's love and compassion have sheltered me through this devastating time, and, though I feel no condemnation, I am humbled by my lack of faith. I know God has so much more for me than drowning in my own self pity. I want to live my life in surrender and gratitude. So I got on my knees in front of my bed and repented (again) for my self pity and lack of trust, and I felt my heart instantly fill with joy, peace and even gratitude. I felt ready to live again. I am so obstinate; so quick to forget the lessons of the past.

No sooner did I get up from my knees than Officer Jones walked into the POD and informed us all to pack up our things to move. As is the usual practice in jail, no more information was given and everyone was left to fret over what they would do to us now. Everyone except me, that is. I was filled with peace, not expecting another blow this time, but expecting that God had a blessing in store for me.

Almost without exception, I have found that once I am truly able to surrender a difficult situation, God moves to improve it. Sure enough, this was no exception. We were moved down the hall to a different POD, this one with individual cells. I was going to have my own space; a room where I could get away from everyone and shut the door. Most of the women cannot bear being locked in a cell for hours at a time, but I do not care much about even leaving my bed most of the time. I was the only one of twenty-five women who was actually glad for the move. Could God have done this just for me? It sure does seem that way. If so, I am in awe of such personal concern. Either way, I may still be in jail, but I feel more content than I have in months.

As I was settling into my new space, I had this crazy thought that maybe I would be better off in here than out in the free world right now anyway. I am so heartbroken and fragile. I am not sure I could bear up under all that I would have to face out there. Only

God knows. I trust Him with my life. I really do. God is good. He has done such a miracle in my heart. I have felt wonderful today. It has been quite a while since I could say that.

Although I am grateful for my little cell, my circumstances really have not changed much. Yet my circumstances do not matter. I am acutely aware of being in God's loving care and even excited about whatever surprises He has in store for me. I feel free that I do not have to worry about anything - my needs are all taken care of. All I have to do is simply rest in Him and go along for the ride.

Everyone else is very upset and stressed about our move. Me? I cannot stop smiling. They can take my journal and everything else I have; they can try to fabricate more charges against me; they can treat me badly. Still, they cannot take what really matters to me. I am loved by the God of the Universe. And He's got me. No matter where I am or what happens, I am safe.

August 15, It Is Done

> *"The Lord doesn't turn His back on people forever.*
> *He might bring suffering, but He will also show loving concern.*
> *How great is His faithful love!*
> *He doesn't want to bring pain or suffering to people."*
> - Lamentations 3:31-33

I woke up at 5:30am, after only five hours of sleep, ready to go. There is so much I want to do today - read, pray, draw, catch up on letters, exercise and encourage these other women. I feel great! I cannot get over what God has done in my heart - He is awesome!

This morning as I prayed words I pray every day - *"I bind the devil and command him to loose my peace, joy and prosperity"* - it hit me. It is done! God has already accomplished that. And if He has done that, then He is surely answering my other prayers as well. I feel confident that this is true. God has more than doubled my faith! Tears of joy came as this revelation hit me in a powerful way: my prayers **are** answered. God is faithful and I am precious to Him.

August 18, Miracles Happen

"God, everything You do is holy.
What god is so great as our God?
You are the God who does miracles?"
- Psalm 77:13

I realized this morning that part of the miracle God did in my heart was that He took away my pain. I still miss my loved ones. I still have deep remorse for the pain they have suffered on my account. I understand that grief is a long slow process. For the moment, however, my grief and sorrow are gone. Knowing my heart can bear only so much, God has lifted it from me. I have been in so much pain for the past year, and now, suddenly, it is gone! I call that a miracle. Only God could have done that.

With my spirits lifted, I am now able to actually enjoy this little vacation from life - no responsibilities, no worries, no pressure. There is nothing I have to do with my time but take care of myself. After years of me taking care of others, usually at my own expense, God is now taking care of me. It may be a harsh environment, and for some it is boring, but I am grateful for this break and I never run out of things to do. If only I could go outside in nature sometimes, or at least see out of a window, I would want for nothing.

They call this punishment, but I know that God is not punishing me. He is protecting me and He is giving me time - time for me, time to heal, time to learn and grow. I am on a much-needed, long overdue sabbatical from life. I am determined that I will make the most of this gift of time and that I will have the last laugh. I have started calling this a resort. Granted it is a one star (maybe even a negative five star), but you get what you pay for.

Most women are so miserable in here. They do not know what to think of my perspective. The grass is always greener on the other side and it is so easy to forget when you are in here just how hard life really is out there in the "free" world. I choose to see the green grass right where I am; even if it is only in a photo!

August 21, Peace Beyond Understanding

"Peace I leave with you. My peace I give you.
I do not give to you as the world gives.
Do not let your hearts be troubled and do not be afraid."
- John 14:27

I am feeling very much at peace. After months (well, actually years) of heartache and suffering, I have overcome and won this battle. I know there will be other battles, but this is a huge victory. I really believe God has delivered me. I am not afraid anymore. There are so many uncertainties in my life, but I feel such a peace that I do not need to worry about any of them. God has it all under control. I can depend on Him to care for me no matter how bad things look.

August 23, In Any Situation

"I know what it is to be in need, and I know what it is to have plenty.
I have learned the secret of being content in any and every situation,
whether well fed or hungry, whether living in plenty or in want.
I can do all things through Christ who strengthens me."
- Philippians 4:12-13

My court date for sentencing is quickly approaching, but I am not worried. As far as getting out of here, I am at peace about it. I will be fine either way. Whatever happens, I am anticipating that God has great blessings for me and I cannot wait to see what they are. Only He knows if I am ready to be out there or not. I am content to stay here and continue my vacation from life and be taken care of until the time is right. I hope I can hold onto this and still feel this way when it is time for court.

August 27, What Next, Papa?

"I am constantly hounded by those who slander me,
and many are boldly attacking me.
But when I am afraid, I will put my trust in you.
I praise God for what He has promised.
I trust in God, so why should I be afraid?

AVERY GARRETT LONG

What can mere mortals do to me?"
- Psalm 56:2-4

Today I was praying and thanking God for the work He has accomplished in my heart - just two weeks ago, though it seems longer. Whatever happens, I am ok with it. I am not afraid of what men can do to me. My faith and trust in God have grown tremendously and I know that whatever the future holds, He wants the best for me. There have been many years of my life that I could not say I honestly believed that. I am actually anticipating His plans for me with the excitement of a child at Christmas. How many people in jail facing a sentencing can say that? That is how great is the miracle that He has given to me.

It occurred to me that God could give me a miracle in my circumstances. He could give me everything I want, but it would not compare. I could and probably would still find things to be miserable about. Instead, He changed my heart, which is so much greater of a miracle, because it is impervious to circumstances. It will enable me to weather any situation and still experience the joy and peace of truly believing in God's love for me. Wow! Now that really is a miracle!

For my whole life it has been so hard for me to completely trust in God's love for me. That trust has grown slowly over the years, but last week, God took me through a quantum leap forward and my doubt is gone. In truth, it is one of those things for which there are no words to fully explain.

August 30, Vessel of Love

"The Lord takes good care of all those who fall.
He lifts up all those who feel helpless...
The Lord stands up for those who are beaten down.
He sets prisoners free."
- Psalm 145:14, 146:3, 7

After becoming furious over the staff's unwillingness to properly care for my young friend Ariana's broken hand, I was thinking about how cruel some humans are to others. I see a great deal of that in here and it is truly sickening. The cruelty of a person really becomes

136

evident when they have a little power over another. While expressing my frustration to God about this, I became very sad about all the hate and abuse in this world and it brought me to bitter tears.

As a strongly empathetic person, I am often overwhelmed by the fact that I am surrounded by hurting people; some of them inmates who have been humbled by their failures and some of them officers whose wounds have turned them into self-righteous bullies. The latter are much harder to love, but, in truth, it is just a different manifestation of the same sickness.

Deep down, we are all the same wounded insecure creatures; all seriously in need of love. I am judged harshly by some, but it doesn't really matter what anyone thinks of me. It has been in my greatest failure that I have come to a much deeper understanding of my worth; I am priceless to the King of All. Not because of anything worthy in me, not because of anything that I have done or not done, but because of who He is - Love.

My greatest desire is to be God's vessel of love and hope to these hurting people, even the cruel ones. This is what gives meaning and purpose to all my suffering. And this is why I am here.

September 4, Hit Me with Your Best Shot

"Knock me down. It's all in vain. I'll get right back up on my feet again."
- Pat Benatar

I was wide awake at 2:00am for no apparent reason. My first thought was, *"They have tried and tried to beat me down in this place, but I just keep getting back up."* This last time, I almost did not get back up, but God renewed my strength. It may not really be "they", as in those in power here. It may actually be my spiritual enemy who hates me and wants to destroy me. Yet I know that God wins, and I will win because I am His.

Today, I received my pre-sentence report in the mail from my lawyer. It was so full of distortions and even outright lies that I began to fall into despair again. I felt my trust, my peace, my acceptance - all that I have gained in these last weeks - slipping. I felt a cold fear hitting me in waves like ice going through my veins. Worst of all, I felt the familiar hopelessness. I tried to accept and honor my feelings rather than fight them, but the agonizing pain returned. I did my best to pray but all I could really manage were cries for help and feelings of failure.

I am angry with myself for being back here again, but that helps nothing. I know who I am and what is in my heart, yet others keep telling me that they know what is in my heart better than me, which only causes me to question myself and feel confused. And scared. I do not know how to endure this agony again. Right now, I cannot imagine ever being free again or ever having a normal life. Nonetheless, I am still standing and that is no small feat.

Chapter 14

David's Tears

"Weep no more. When He hears your cry of despair,
He will indeed show you mercy;
when He hears it, He will respond to you."
- Isaiah 30:19

"The Lord is close to the brokenhearted
and saves those who are crushed in spirit."
- Psalm 34:18

September 11, Control

"They do not fear bad news;
they confidently trust the LORD to care for them."
- Psalm 112:7

I began my day with an attack of dread and fear over my upcoming court date. I prayed against this attack. Still I could not shake these feelings. The truth is that it is scarier for me to be released from jail than it is to stay, so I am not sure why I should worry about court. It just makes me feel so vulnerable to have my deepest feelings of the past six months just "out there" for anyone to read. This is just one of the many ways that I have no control over my life. Then again, while I may have felt more a sense of control before I was incarcerated, it is actually only an illusion. Even when we believe we are in control, we really are not.

So all I can do is rest assured that God is in control. And

remember that my life matters to Him.

September 13, Just a Dream

"They have broken my heart. It has left me helpless....
I'm in pain. I'm in deep trouble.
God, save me and keep me safe...
The Lord hears those who are in need.
He doesn't forget His people in prison."
- Psalm 69:20, 29, 33

I woke up this morning sobbing from a dream about being rejected from my family. Knowing that this is not just a dream, but a reality did not help me to feel better. It took me a long time to stop crying and calm down. While I have done some healing, there is still so much hurt in my heart.

My court date is quickly approaching and I am very emotional. I am having a lot of anxiety, as well as the same racing heart and shaky feeling I had when my breakdown began last fall. I still have mixed feelings about getting out. I suppose that I might possibly find the strength to rebuild my life, but I do not know if I feel strong enough to deal with all the judgment and the broken relationships I will face out there. And I am dreading that. I am trying not to jump ahead, but to just take one step at a time. I know that no matter what happens, this will be a stressful, challenging week. I just want to be done with it.

The only way to get through this is to remember who is really in charge of my life and hold on to His peace. That is the only way I can handle my life because my problems are far too big for me. How does anyone survive this life without God? I would have given up long ago.

September 14, Who I am

"You have seen what is in my heart. You know all about me."
- Psalm 139:1

After pouring my heart out to God for a long time last night, I began to feel my peace returning and slept amazingly well. I spent a long time praying again this morning. I recognize that I went back to worrying about what people think instead of continuing to trust in God's love and good will for me. None of these people judging me can define me. I do know who I am, and it does not matter what anyone else thinks. More importantly, God knows my heart and that is all that matters. I made the choice again to trust Him and go back to acceptance of what is, and slowly my emotions stabilized.

Tomorrow I have court. I am nervous about possibly having to take the stand but I am at peace with whatever the outcome. My life is in God's hands. He knows what I can bear.

September 15, More Than I Can Bear

> *"LORD, how long must I wait? Will you forget me forever?*
> *How long will you turn your face away from me?*
> *How long must I struggle with my thoughts?*
> *How long must my heart be sad day after day?*
> *How long will my enemies keep winning the battle over me?*
> *LORD my God, look at me and answer me.*
> *Give me new life, or I will die.*
> *Then my enemies will say, 'We have beaten her.'*
> *They will be filled with joy when I die."*
> - Psalm 13:1-4

I cannot help but feel abandoned by God. I thought He promised not to give me more than I can bear. What does it mean? All these messages I thought He had been giving me of hope that things were going to get better; that I was almost to the end of my suffering. Am I delusional? I am really angry with God right now anyway. What good is it to live a life faithful and devoted to Him when all I get for it is pain? You know, that is exactly how I was feeling when I got into this relationship that has destroyed my life. Now I will pay for it for the rest of my life.

It's not as much the three year prison sentence followed by ten years of probation, even though my clean record and guidelines of no jail time were completely dismissed. What is insufferable to me is the thought of spending my entire life registering as a **violent** sex offender. It's such a lie and the judge knew it, but he did not care. Without so much as a glance at my anguished eyes and gaunt, despondent frame, he callously annihilated me. My cries for help were ignored. It's just politics to them. My life is unimportant. Just another pawn in their game.

I thought I was prepared to accept whatever happened, but I have no idea how to accept this. Some of my girls will probably get married, even maybe have kids, while I am locked up. My life is destroyed. I have nothing to hope for. How do I motivate myself to get up everyday? For what? To sit around in a room with no purpose, no point to my life and no future? I feel completely hopeless. How can I pick myself back up this time? My friends came to try to console me - even Officer Jones tried to cheer me up - but I am inconsolable.

September 19, Ocean of Pain

"When I was in deep trouble, I searched for the Lord.
All night long I prayed, with hands lifted toward heaven,
but my soul was not comforted. I think of God,
and I moan, overwhelmed with longing for His help.
You don't let me sleep. I am too distressed even to pray!
I think of the good old days, long since ended,
when my nights were filled with joyful songs.
I search my soul and ponder the difference now.
Has the Lord rejected me forever?
Will He never again be kind to me?
Is His unfailing love gone forever?
Have His promises permanently failed?
Has God forgotten to be gracious?
Has He slammed the door on His compassion?
And I said, 'This is my fate;
the Most High has turned His hand against me.'"
- Psalm 77:2-10

I shut down again; staying in bed and not eating, refusing to talk to anyone. I even refused to see the counselor when he came to see me, and I have been waiting months to see him. A river of tears poured down my face as I was taken to be fingerprinted for the sex offender registry. Despair is devouring me.

Many people, inmates and a few officers, checked on me today, trying to encourage me. I appreciated the efforts and tried to be polite, but I just want everyone to leave me alone. The officers keep asking if I think I will hurt myself. I would not tell them if I would, but I know that it is not my right to take my life. For what it's worth, my life belongs to God.

I do feel so hopeless about my life. I cannot see any light at the end of the tunnel. Just pain, pain, and more pain. I am tired of pain and I am tired of life. I cannot think of anything to look forward to other than more pain and I just want to lay down and quit.

September 30, Grieving My Losses

"My heart is sick, withered like grass, and I have lost my appetite.
Because of my groaning, I am reduced to skin and bones.
I lie awake, lonely as a solitary bird on the roof.
My tears run down into my drink because of Your anger and wrath.
For You have picked me up and thrown me out.
I am withering away like grass...
Look down to earth from heaven to hear the groans of the prisoners...
God, save me. My troubles are like a flood. I'm up to my neck in them.
I'm sinking in deep mud. I have no firm place to stand.
I am out in deep water. The waves roll over me.
I'm worn out from calling for help...
You know how foolish I've been. My guilt is not hidden from You...
God, answer me because You love me so much.
Save me, as You always do."
- Psalm 69 and 102

I am grieving my many losses; all my loved ones, especially my children, not being there for them, missing so much, the separation. Everyone I love has turned away from me and I feel so alone. God is all I have, though I have been struggling with so many questions and doubts again.

I pray through my many tears, pouring out my pain to the only One who can truly understand. I ask how much He is going to put me through. Is it ever going to stop? Will I ever have enough suffering to satisfy Him? Is He going to break me totally? I know I have been feeling sorry for myself and wish I could be stronger. I do not really believe God wants me to suffer or causes my suffering. I asked His forgiveness and prayed for help accepting my lot.

Once again, I have jumped ahead and worried instead of trusting God to provide for me. Still, even in the midst of so much heartbreak, I can see the many ways He is lovingly providing for me. I can see that, even in this bleak place, He is sheltering me from what might truly be more than I could bear. I may waver, doubt, return to old thinking patterns, but He is faithful, steady and true. And fortunately, **ever so** patient with me.

October 4, Trusting

> *"But Jesus didn't trust them, because he knew human nature."*
> - John 2:24

I read in my devotional book today an admonition to rely on God alone. I really want to trust God and accept His will for me, but I feel panicked about the thought of spending more months in this concrete room 24/7. I know that I cannot trust in people. All people will let me down, just as I let people down. Only God is faithful. Only in Him can I put my trust.

I must forgive those who have hurt, abandoned, and betrayed me, just as Christ has forgiven me. I have to make that choice daily, because I have been hurt so badly by so many. It is my choice, though, because I want nothing in my heart to separate me from God.

I keep surrendering my wounded heart to God. I believe He will heal it. I can love others even if I cannot depend on or trust in them. I understand that no one owes me anything and that I need to let go of expectations of others. I am working on that attitude. At least I recognize it, and can see that it is just my huge ego talking and not the true me. Still, though surrounded by people, I feel so alone. I may feel alone, but I am **not** alone. He is with me. Always.

October 9, Have Mercy

"My sadness has worn me out.
Give me strength as you have promised.
I have chosen to be faithful to You. Don't let me be put to shame.
You have set my heart free...You have given me hope.
Even when I suffer, I am comforted because
You promised to keep me alive...
Lord, You are everything I need.
I have looked to You with all my heart.
Be kind to me as You have promised."
- Psalm 119

There seems to be no end to the struggles. I tried again to retrieve my stolen journal but it appears that I will not be getting it back and I have no idea where it has gone. I know by their comments and dirty looks that some of the officers have read parts of it and are unhappy with the things I have written about this place. I suspect that is why it disappeared. Sorry if the truth offends them but they had no business reading my diary in the first place. It has probably been destroyed by now, but it is a very uneasy feeling knowing it could fall into anyone's hands. I even wondered if excerpts of it might turn up in the paper. It would not surprise me. Yet another thing I have to surrender to God.

At first, I felt so desperate and overwhelmed; that turned into my old companions *hopelessness* and *despair*. Exhausted by all the heartache and injustice of my life, I thought how badly I wish I could just get off this "ride". I do not know how much more God expects me to take. I pray for mercy.

October 10, Bottle of Tears

"You keep track of all my sorrows.
You have collected all my tears in your bottle.

145

You have recorded each one in your book."
- Psalm 56:8

Still feeling so discouraged today, I tried to take my eyes off me and encourage others. I spoke with a few women in the POD who I know are hurting, and, after speaking to each of them, I went back to my room to pray for them. I began to cry and could not stop. There is so much pain in this place; so many hurting women and it breaks my heart. I grieve not only for my own losses, but for theirs as well. The burdens are more than I can carry, so I must put them in my Father's hands.

October 15, Bleeding Love

"He heals the broken hearted and bandages their wounds."
- Psalm 147:3

I feel so unlovable; rejected by everyone. *"Am I even lovable to you, Lord?"* My poor heart is so worn out from pain. Is life always going to hurt this much? If so, I do not want to stick around for much more of it.

I do not want to become bitter and hard, but I know that I cannot trust anyone here. I know they are very wounded women and I try to keep my heart open to showing them God's love, but the drama drives me crazy - even though I do my best to stay out of it.

Sometimes I really think I should just get put in Segregation. If I could have my radio and coffee in there, I would have probably done that long ago. Yet, deep down, I know that God has put me with these women for a reason.

I believe that my Mika-Maka literally died of a broken heart. Just a little over a year after Mom's death, Mika-Maka's heart just split open and she hemorrhaged to death. I know the kind of pain she must have been feeling in her heart. Sometimes I feel sure that my heart will split in two, and I have to admit it would be a relief. I wonder how much more my poor bleeding heart can take.

Chapter 15

Tender Mercies

*"Remember, Lord, Your tender mercies and Your gracious love;
indeed, they are eternal!"*
- Psalm 25:6

October 21, I Don't Mind

*"For whoever wants to save their life will lose it,
but whoever loses their life for Me will find it."* (Jesus)
- Matthew 16:25

My first thought this morning was that I have to let it all go -
again; my journal, my divorce, my future. Give it all to God to take
care of and stop trying to rescue myself or look to other people to
rescue me. I know; I have been here before; many times, actually. I
am sure there will be many more. This is one of the great lessons of
my life - **letting go**. Surrender to God. All my attempts to help
myself have failed anyway and every person I have looked to to meet
my needs has let me down at some point.

I sense God calling me to lay it all down again - give it all to
Him. Again. It feels like stepping right off a cliff, but I am going to
trust Him to catch me. What have I got to lose really? I have done a
pretty lousy job of running my own life anyway. God certainly could
do no worse. I think it is time to go for it. It is time to truly start
living like *I don't mind what happens.* I know I still will mind at times,
but I am going to try to stop resisting and let whatever will be be. I
might as well, because the truth is that it will whether I "let" it or not.

It comes back to surrender **every time**.

October 24, Scary Thoughts

"The Lord saves me. Evening, morning and noon,
I cry out in distress,and He hears my voice.
He rescues me unharmed from the battle waged against me,
even though many oppose me."
- Psalm 55:16-18

I want to hide in my bed all the time, but I am not giving in to that longing. I am spending more time praying and meditating, so I am not plagued by my thoughts. My thoughts are scary. I cannot handle them, because my future is so scary. All my relationships are ruined. My heart is so broken. If I let myself dwell on it all, it will destroy me. So I fix my eyes on Jesus. It is the only way I can survive.

November 2, Light in the Dark

"Feed the hungry, and help those in trouble.
Then your light will shine out from the darkness,
and the darkness around you will be as bright as noon."
- Isaiah 58:10

A young woman in our POD was assaulted by another woman today. Though we called for help, it was a full ten minutes before Officer Dodge showed up. All she did was threaten to lock us in our cells if we did not quiet down. Therefore, no one said anything, knowing it would only get us in trouble. Once again, I fumed at the injustice in this jail. I spent an hour praying and meditating before I was able to calm down and fully surrender it to God.

At times, it is so hard to cope with the terrible way we are treated here. There are a few decent officers, but there are many more who feel superior and look down on us. I guess a lot of it is because, although God looks at the heart, people only judge others by the outside. I am so glad God sees our hearts...and even more glad that He loves us in spite of the sinfulness in them.

I know that darkness prevails in this place - in this world - and that I cannot change it. I can become cynical or I can rise above and be a light in the darkness. That is what I choose. To be His light in this dark place. Even though I am weak, I pray He will accomplish this through me.

November 19, Overflowing Comfort

"Blessed be the God and Father of our Lord Jesus Christ,
The Father of compassion and the God of all comfort,
who comforts us in all our troubles, so that we can comfort those
in any trouble with the comfort we ourselves have received from God.
For just as the sufferings of Christ overflow to us,
So also through Christ our comfort overflows."
- II Corinthians 1:4

I have a new cellmate. She is a young mother of three small children named Isabella. She is originally from Columbia and speaks very little English. She is so scared, because, as an illegal immigrant, she is likely to be deported and separated from her children. I tried to make her comfortable and assure her the best I could. God always seems to find a way to keep me going by sending someone to help and get my mind off me.

Isabella is quiet and sweet and I am grateful to have her with me. When she got off the phone with her sister earlier, she was crying, so I sat with her, hugged her and let her cry on my shoulder. My heart goes out to her. I feel helpless, knowing I can do nothing for her but offer comfort and understanding. Isabella and I are getting more comfortable with one another and I am grateful for such a great roommate. We are already praying together. I was even comfortable enough to cry in front of her today. She hugged me and reminded me that the Lord is with me. I have started teaching her English and it is so fun to have a practical way that I can help her. I really am happiest when I can help others who are hurting rather than thinking of my own pain. It is great to feel useful and it gives me some purpose to my empty life.

It is beautiful when we women take care of one another, although many are too busy backstabbing and causing drama. I wish they could all understand that united we stand, divided we fall. In spite of the users and manipulators I have met, though, I am grateful for the special women God has brought into my life through this experience.

December 31, Let It Pour

New Year's Eve. After a year in jail, I have finally been moved to prison. I begin this new year with a heart of gratitude for all the little things that I used to take for granted. At 3:30am, I woke up and looked out my window to see it start pouring. A window! Rain! I have had neither of those luxuries for a year. To feel the rain falling on me as I walked to breakfast was a big thrill. I have dreamed about this moment for months. Everything is special now after living in a concrete cage for so long. Everything is new. It is almost like being a child again and discovering the wonder of the world for the first time.

January 6, First Moon

I saw my first full moon at 3:00am this morning as I walked to the chow hall for breakfast. It was a little bit behind the clouds, but still bright enough and so very beautiful. It is such a joy to be able to walk outside every day. I may not get to choose when I go out and I may still be behind tall razor-wire fences, but I feel so free.

January 10, Healing Hands

"Help carry each other's burdens. In this way you will follow Christ's teachings."
- Galatians 6:2

I feel like I am not carrying my burdens alone anymore. There are people who actually care about me and affirm me. After being torn down so much in the past year, it really is healing to be built up. It is a shame I had to be incarcerated to be valued by others. God is working through these women to love and care for me; and to give me hope. Tonight I go to bed with a full tummy and a feeling that God has me.

January 25, Eternal Gifts

"So we do not lose heart. Though our outer self is wasting away,
our inner self is being renewed day by day.
For our light and temporary affliction is producing for us
an eternal glory that far outweighs our troubles."
- 2 Corinthians 4:16-17

I enjoyed a leisurely private coffee time with my Father and spent time thanking Him for all His blessings in my life. In spite of all the hardship of this past year, I am so grateful for the experience. All the people that I have gotten to know, learning to depend entirely on God, learning to appreciate every little thing that I once took for granted, the "time out" from life to take care of myself. So many great lessons that I could have learned no other way and so many incredible experiences I would have missed had I stayed on my normal, predictable path. I cried tears of love and thankfulness to God for this journey He has taken me on and for His great love for me - as undeserving as I am. When I concentrate on these things instead of the negative, I can be excited about my life and look forward to God's surprises for me in the future.

January 28, Freely Received, Freely Given

"Live a life filled with love, following the example of Christ.
His love was not cautious but extravagant.
He didn't love in order to get something from us
but to give everything of Himself to us.
Love like that."
- Ephesians 5:2

God reminded me of how freely He has given to me, always providing generously to me. In turn, it is only right that I share what He has given me. Whether I believe a person to be a user or not should not change what I give. No matter what they are after, those who use and manipulate really just need love and kindness, given without any strings or games. I can only gain by sharing no matter the intentions of others. Yes, there are always those who take advantage of a generous spirit, but if I keep my heart open to loving others in whatever way God leads me, I can trust Him to take care of me as well as give me the discernment I need. Besides, I have learned how very little I really do need.

I have seen many people leave with nothing, no one and nowhere to go. Actually, I will leave with no one and nowhere to go, but hopefully I will not be totally destitute. I guess there is no better way to learn empathy for people than to have some understanding of what it is like to walk in their shoes. If I someday have the opportunity to help other women rebuild their lives, these trials will certainly enable me to relate. Another hidden gem in this mess.

February 5, Snow!

> *"The heavens declare the glory of God;*
> *the skies proclaim the work of his hands."*
> - Psalm 19:1

I woke up to snow! It was beautiful. I enjoyed watching it snow all morning as I drank coffee and made cards to send to my children. When I am finally able to freely enjoy nature as much as I want, I do not think I could ever take it for granted again. It is never more apparent than when you lose it that the beauty of this world is one of God's greatest gifts.

Chapter 16

Through the Fire

*"These trials will show that your faith is genuine.
It is being tested as fire tests and purifies gold--
though your faith is far more precious than mere gold.
So when your faith remains strong through many trials,
it may result in praise, glory and honor when Jesus Christ is revealed."*
- 1 Peter 1:7

February 9, Depressing Prospects

"Blessed are those who are sad. They will be comforted."
- Matthew 5:4

I had a lot of trouble getting to sleep last night with so much on my mind. This morning, I woke up sobbing from another distressing dream. I have been having a lot of them lately. I am feeling so hopeless about my life again. I have been having troubling thoughts about the barriers stacked against me and beginning to doubt myself again. I feel so alone, so sad about all my relationships, especially with my kids.

My future is terrifying to me and I am overwhelmed with all the things I will one day have to face. Spending my life being labeled a child molester and a violent criminal is an incredibly depressing prospect. Too much to face. It is excruciating. Life in here has only been a small taste and already I feel like crawling in a hole and dying. Defending myself only makes it worse.

Feeling deeply troubled, I spent time praying and attempting to release my burdens to God. Praying helped a little. Later, in an effort to break my cycle of wallowing in self-pity, I forced myself to come out of my cave to attend a church service. It was an uplifting service and the chaplain preached a very relevant sermon about "*waiting on the Lord*", after which I was able to partake in my first Communion in over a year. I really felt God's peaceful presence. It was just what I needed to lift my spirits and escape the chaos for bit.

February 12, What is Normal?

"Those who look to Him are radiant, and their faces shall never be ashamed."
- Psalm 34:5

For as long as I can remember, I have been told by the men in my life that something is wrong with me; I am not ok; I am not normal. I am the problem. No matter what the problem is. As I berated myself for all the ways I have failed my family, I wondered if maybe they are right. Maybe I am the problem. Maybe I am a monster. Maybe I am crazy.

I have just made a big mess of my life. I felt so much pain in my heart as I thought about all of this and I could not stop crying for a long time. The sad thing is that I have always tried so hard to do the right thing and treat others the way I want to be treated. Yet, somehow I have completely failed. Maybe it is understandable that my family wants nothing to do with me.

In this pressure cooker, no matter how hard I try to love others, I always seem to have conflicts. There is a great deal of frustration and anger here and it brings out the worst in people. All the strife returns me to an old wound - to the old questions. Maybe something *is* wrong with me. Maybe it *is* my fault. Maybe once people get to know me, they will not (do not) like me. Maybe I really am <u>not</u> ok. However, there is a new voice growing stronger in my head that says maybe it does not matter. Maybe it is time to stop beating myself up. Maybe the only one I need to be ok with is the One who made me just the way I am. Maybe I do not need to drive myself crazy with all this self doubt anymore. Then again, if I already am crazy, no worries, right?

"But by the grace of God I am what I am." (1 Corinthians 15:10)

March 6, Not Over Yet

> *"Do not sob anymore. Do not let tears fall from your eyes.*
> *I will reward you for your work, announces the Lord.*
> *Your children will return from the land of the enemy.*
> *So I am giving you hope for the years to come.*
> *Your children will return to their own land."*
> - Jeremiah 31:16-17

God is so amazing! I cannot doubt that He spoke to me this morning. I was looking up a verse in Jeremiah (31:3-4) and this verse on the other page just jumped out at me. It is definitely a very clear, direct promise. At this point, my twenty-four years of work seem wasted. Yet He says He will reward me for it. In spite of how things look, I will believe it. His promises are true.

March 14, For Better or Worse

> *"Since He himself has gone through suffering and testing,*
> *He is able to help us when we are being tested."*
> - Hebrews 2:18

I spent the whole morning in my room enjoying time alone with God. As I considered the fact that God does allow us to suffer even though He loves us, I realized that I use this as an excuse to hold onto my fears of the future. There is no guarantee that my life will get any better. It could get worse. More bad things could happen. Trusting in God offers me no assurances of an easy life; often quite the opposite. Therefore, I have been living in fear of what may be lying around the next corner to attack.

I asked God's forgiveness for my lack of faith. As I prayed to learn contentment no matter what my circumstances, I had to admit that there is one circumstance in my life that I do not know how to accept - separation from my children. They are such a part of me and

I have no idea how to ever be content with that. Thinking of the way I have let them down and all that I am missing in their lives is heart-wrenching. I let myself feel that deep pain and the release of tears. Knowing that there is nothing I can do to change these circumstances or how I feel, all I can do is relinquish it once again.

Some people pay a big price for their mistakes, and some people do not pay at all (in this life anyway). Some of us have to learn our lessons the hard way, yet I would rather learn the hard way than not learn at all. As tough as this time has been for me, I would still rather learn to trust God than to continue trusting in myself or others. I would rather be forced to recognize that I am not in control than live under the deception that I am. I suppose the only way to learn to fully release the reins is when you have absolutely no choice. Therefore, my suffering is not in vain. It always has a purpose.

March 23, Not Ready

Everyone is talking about the possibility of a law passing that would reduce the time served on a sentence. I hope it is true for some of these women, but, for me, it does not much matter. It would only make a few months difference and, as crazy as it sounds, I am so **not** ready to leave here. I have nowhere to go, no money, and no support, so maybe I am better off in prison. I do not want to face the world out there alone.

April 4, Idols

"Jesus turned and told them, 'Anyone who comes to me but refuses to let go of father, mother, spouse, children, brothers, sisters— yes, even one's own self!—can't be my disciple.' "
- Luke 14:26

I had an appointment with the Chaplain this morning. I have been meeting with her every two weeks for counseling. It is one of the few things I have to look forward to these days. I talked about how I have been feeling, about my fear of being released and the feeling that I could not face life without my children. Her insightful response had a powerful impact on me.

In the most loving and nonjudgmental way, she explained to me that I was making an idol of my children and that my thinking was a bit co-dependent. She reminded me that *all* I need in order to be ok is God. I did not feel condemned, but I did feel convicted. God has been teaching me this in so many ways, but I never thought about it including my kids, because, after all, a mother should not be alienated from her children. Doesn't God always want reconciliation? Well, yes, but this is not my choice at this point. How can I be alright with it? Because it is not within my power to change. I sensed God's voice in the Chaplain's message to me. She went on to encourage me that this is the time to find out who Avery is besides being a mother and caregiver to others, because that is not all that I am. I am not sure that I have ever fully taken the time to find out who I am beyond that. Now is the time to discover myself and pursue my dreams.

I left her office feeling so encouraged and awed by what God showed me through her exhortations. Of course, it is so obvious. The message God has been giving me for years now is that He is all I need. He has been stripping me of all my idols and maybe my kids are the last holdouts. I justify to myself that I am their mom and they need me, right? Then where are they? Is it about their need of me or my need to be needed by them? I have suffered over this long enough and I cannot let it destroy me. I love them all very much; they will always be part of me. However, right now my children do not need or want me in their lives, so I must accept that and move on. I will give what I have to give to those who want it. There are so many people desperate for mother love. All I can do is continue to pray for my children and keep my heart open to them. Only by His strength.

I love when God opens my eyes. This is what I pray for every day and this is an answer to my prayers. I feel like a burden has lifted. I am slowly letting go of all those things that I have been trying to control and giving them to God. Each step of this yielding brings a deeper peace to my soul.

April 13, Learning Obedience

"(Jesus) learned obedience from what He suffered."
- Hebrews 5:8

As painful as it has been, I believe I am blessed for all the trials that God has allowed in my life. Through it all, He has taught me lessons in surrender, humility, and obedience. Some things are learned no other way than through suffering. Even Jesus learned obedience from His suffering, though He was without sin, because there is no true obedience without the temptation to disobey. That must be why we are drawn to Jesus when we are suffering, because He knows. He has been there. He did not have to, but He wanted to experience all that we experience. He wanted to feel our pain. He made that choice because He loves us that much. He has the scars to prove it.

I also find myself drawn to others who carry the scars of battle. I have developed a strong connection with some of these women that I have met in here. There is an intimacy that is found between those who have been through the fire. These are the ones who have learned wisdom the hard way. Those who have never failed cannot as readily understand the depth of their own sinfulness nor the need for God's grace. From my point of view, that is when you truly begin to live.

April 26, Wasted Years

"For we are God's masterpiece. He has created us anew in Christ Jesus, so we can do the good things he planned for us long ago."
- Ephesians 2:10

I have hopes and dreams for my future, which I believe God has put in my heart, but it sometimes seems as though they will never come to pass. With time ticking by and with so much I want to do, I often feel that I am wasting my life sitting in prison. At times, I lose hope that I will ever get there. Yet God is showing me that He is working to bring much good out of these "wasted" years. He promises to take the pieces of my destroyed life and work miracles. This is not a speedy process and I realize that I must be patient. It

158

has taken many years and many wounds to reach this broken state and it will take time for God to heal my heart.

Being purified through the fire is a painful process, but I know it is the only way to produce a true inner transformation. I have heard it said that the more intense the fire, the greater the destiny. If so, then I must have an incredible destiny! It would definitely take a huge miracle to put my life back together, but, thankfully, I believe in a God of miracles. Once again, my part is merely to submit and try to stay out of the way. It will all happen. In His time, not mine.

Chapter 17

Wonder-working Power

"There is power, power, wonder-working power,
in the precious blood of the Lamb."

"Who can separate us from Christ's love?
Can trouble or hard times or harm or hunger?
Can nakedness or danger or war?
No! In all these things we are more than conquerors
through Christ Jesus who loves us."
- Romans 8:35, 37

May 5, The Vision

"I did not receive it from any man, nor was I taught it;
rather, I received it by revelation from Jesus Christ."
- Galatians 1:12

I was expecting a quiet, uneventful day spent mostly in bed. I was surprised when Officer Davitt called over my speaker to tell me that I had a visit. Since visits are rare for me and Davitt has a strong foreign accent, I thought he was speaking to my roommate. Once he clarified that he meant me, I quickly got ready and rushed down to the atrium where Davitt greeted me with a curt, *"Not you!"* He unapologetically claimed to have made a mistake. Since this officer always seems to be looking for ways to give me a hard time, I suspected that his mistake was intentional.

Having difficulty managing my disappointment, I became angry with Davitt for getting my hopes up for nothing. I rudely snapped at him, *"You need to learn how to speak English!"* All the stress and cruelty here has been starting to get to me and, admittedly, I was looking for a fight.

Davitt sent me to the holding cell for being disrespectful. He was right - I was being disrespectful; not nearly as disrespectful as he treats inmates, but I know it was still wrong of me. At the time, I just did not care and I told him so as I cheerfully headed off to receive my punishment.

The tears I held back began to fall the minute I entered the holding cell. It has been four months since I had a visit and my emotions were severely jerked around by the let down. I was actually so relieved to be alone for awhile. I needed the privacy for a good cry that I did not have to repress. I tried to share my feelings with God, but had difficulty finding the words to express them. That is the wonderful thing about God; He already understands without me needing to say a word. It was very challenging to do, but I finally managed to go through each area where I was struggling, and one-by-one, surrender each to Him.

Eventually, I was able to calm down. Then, I noticed something I had not heard in a long time - SILENCE!! Beautiful, blessed silence! It was music to my poor, tired ears. I enjoyed every minute of peace and quiet that I had in that little cell. It was great to be able to cry freely and loudly. I could meditate in actual silence, get on my knees and truly pray alone, and just lay there and listen (to nothing!).

As I was trying to meditate, but feeling so much pain inside, I said, *"God, it hurts so much and I'm afraid it's just a bottomless pit of pain that will never all be gone."* That is when I had a powerful, incredible vision that I will never forget, yet cannot adequately explain either.

I saw a terrified little girl (yes, me) facing that pit. God took her by the hand and said, *"You are not alone. I will go with you into your pit of pain."* The little girl held tightly onto His hand as they faced the pit together - a black, sticky puddle, like tar.

God encouraged her to walk toward it but she was so afraid. *"It's ok. We'll walk through it together,"* He urged. Still she hesitated.

"Will you carry me?" she timidly asked. Immediately, He picked her up and she buried her face in His chest, hiding.

"I want you to look, Avery."

"But, I'm so scared, Daddy."

"Trust me, I've got you." Reluctantly, little Avery turned and faced her fear, as her Father jumped right into that mess. To her surprise, however, instead of being suffocated in a hot tarlike substance, she watched the tar turn white as they fell down, down, down...

They fell for a very long time. Avery noticed that the white "walls" they were plummeting past had words written on them. Though she could not read any of them, she understood that each stone named a specific wound of her life - these stones were what made up the pit. Finally they landed at the bottom.

"You see," God exclaimed. *"There IS a bottom! And we are going to start here, at the bottom, and go up, rather than from the top down. So this way, you will know there's an end and you don't get discouraged."* Then He showed her her very first wounds. These were wounds that she had never remembered, even though they had always been there. They came from her mother. This she had not expected and it surprised her.

She was able to recognize, for the first time, that her father was the one that spent more time with her as a baby. When Avery was just two years old, her mother was sick, almost dying, in the hospital for months after her sister was born. This was the first time she had felt abandoned by her mother, and even though her mother had no choice, that was something a little two year old could not understand. All she knew was that her mother was no longer there for her.

God put out His arms, and one by one, had Avery hand to Him each brick of pain, knowing it was too much for her to carry. As the pile in His arms grew, He explained to her, *"It's too much for you, but for Me it is easy to carry."* As He said this, the huge stack of bricks dissolved into one tiny little box that sat in the palm of His hand. *"You see, it's not much for me at all. That is why you need to let Me carry it. You cannot handle it, but I can."* He picked her back up and they flew to the top of the pit again.

As I opened my eyes, I realized that the heavy weight on my chest was gone...for now...one down...???? to go..."*Thanks, God!*" I exclaimed. That was amazing and awesome!

I asked to stay in the holding cell for as long as they could let me and, when my time was up, I floated calmly back to my building. I hated to return to the chaos, but I was grateful for this brief escape.

As I passed by, I thanked Davitt for the quiet time alone and he just shrugged his shoulders. Everyone was shocked that I had been sent to the holding cell, since I never usually cause any trouble. To some, being alone is a fate worse than death. However, like Brer Rabbit, I had the last laugh. "*Pleeeease, whatever you do, don't throw me in that briar patch!!*" (Side note: What Brer Rabbit's punisher did not know is that he grew up in the briar patch.).

I could not believe it when someone told me that I had been gone for three hours. Time really does fly when you're having fun. Maybe more accurately, time really does fly when you are in the presence of such Great Love.

May 12, I Hear You

> "*I know that the Lord is always with me.*
> *He is at my right hand. I will always be secure.*
> *So my heart is glad. Joy is on my tongue.*
> *My body also will be secure.*
> *You will not leave me in the grave.*
> *You will not let Your faithful one rot away.*
> *You always show me the path that leads to life.*
> *You will fill me with joy when I am with You.*
> *You will give me endless pleasures at Your right hand.*"
> - Psalm 16:8-11

My vision in the holding cell has had a powerful effect on my confidence that I do indeed hear God's voice. I also feel more confident that His promises to work in wondrous ways in my life are real. Now, when God speaks to me, I am not questioning His voice, but instead, my heart is instantly calmed by it.

May 17, Vultures

"The world and its desires pass away,
but whoever does the will of God lives forever."
- I John 2:17

Being incarcerated makes you vulnerable to all the vultures that
swoop in to take advantage while you are helpless to do anything
about it. Ironically, it has been mostly the respected members of
society and those I trusted who have taken advantage of my situation.
Yet God reminds me that things and money do not matter. I have
learned how little I actually need and I know that God will take care
of all my needs. I refuse to waste any energy resenting the injustice of
thieves who prosper from my misfortune, because in truth, I am **far**
richer than they are in the things that matter.

May 24, Pure Ego

"God, see what is in my heart. Know what is there.
Put me to the test. Know what I am thinking.
See if there is anything in my life that You don't like.
Help me to always live right."
- Psalm 139:23-24

In my time with God this morning, He convicted me about the
focus on self, the tendency to blame others for my unhappiness, and
the importance of being centered on God instead. I realized that even
the preoccupation with being "transformed" to be like Christ has had
some ego involved. It relates to my perfectionist tendencies and,
while I have recognized that I cannot accomplish perfectionism, I
have desperately wanted God to make me perfect and feel discontent
until I can reach that state.

Yes, I do want to glorify God and be a vessel of His love in this
world. However, I realized that some of my motivation is pure ego -
a desire to look good to others and be highly esteemed. This is
especially true when I feel discontent with where He has me today. It
comes back to humility again. Rather than thinking with my ego and
worrying about how others see me, it is more crucial to know that

who and "where" I am is just where He wants me to be at this
moment.

June 7, My Identity

"When you look into your heart, you see what you are really like."
- Proverbs 27:19

This morning I had some revelations about myself. I realized
that I am grappling with my identity because I do not believe anyone
needs me. My identity has always been wrapped around being needed
by others. Who am I if no one needs me? I am about to find out. I
am working on freeing myself from this need to be needed and
learning to be ok with taking care of my own needs. There will always
be plenty of time to take care of others, as there always has been, but
this time for me is a very rare gift. I need to relax and enjoy it.

I have such a hard time not feeling selfish and guilty when I feel
I am not helping others or being productive. I know I need to learn
to let go of that and be kind to myself. It seems so easy but it is a
tough lesson for me. I have spent my whole life putting me aside to
take care of others. Since it has come at such a great cost, it is
important that I get this down. I need to take care of me. I matter
just as much as anyone else. Being a loving person means loving
myself too. Today is my mom's birthday and I know she would
appreciate knowing that I am finally grasping what she tried to get
across to me for so many years.

I have had to admit to myself that I still care far more than I
would like about being appreciated by people, even in here. Gradually
I am learning, however, that there is much more to me than what I
do for others. Once again, I return to this truth: I already have the
only approval and appreciation that I need if I just look within. Why
is that so hard to embrace?

June 11, Mind Power

*"Blessed is she who has believed that
the Lord would fulfill His promises to her!"*
- Luke 1:45

I have lately been more aware of the power my thoughts have over my peace of mind. Whenever I catch my mind wandering with upsetting thoughts and worries, I make a conscious effort to turn my attention to God's promises and all my blessings. I have been making a list of the promises in the Bible that are most relevant to me. I want to remember them. Our Bible study teacher said there are 3000 of them. I just need a few really.

When I found myself feeling down this afternoon, I made a short gratitude list:

1) I am NOT alone; God is always with me.

2) At this very present moment, I have no worries and my life is just fine.

3) I have already survived **much** worse than my current circumstances.

4) Good things are coming for me.

5) Tonight, after four months of waiting, I am finally able to start the Meditation

Class (See? Already good things are happening for me.).

Even through the most trying times and in the harshest environments, there are always things to be grateful for if you are looking for them.

June 26, God's Surprise

Two days ago, a thought popped into my head: *"I have a really big surprise for you!"* I was not sure if this thought was coming for God or just me. Not wanting to set myself up for disappointment, I tried not to give it much weight. This afternoon, however, when I was called for an unexpected visit, I wondered if this was my *"surprise"*.

My visitor was a previous co-worker who has been faithfully writing and supporting me for the past few months. I was happy to see her and enjoyed our time together. The real surprise came, however, when she invited me to come live with her husband and her when I get out. They want to come pick me up from prison and bring me home with them, where I will have my own little apartment upstairs. She welcomed me to stay as long as I need to get on my feet.

To this point, I had been looking at shelters and half-way houses since I had nowhere to go, so this was a great relief. I was deeply touched by their generous offer. I was also very moved when I recognized that God had indeed spoken to me to let me know this was His work. Another reassuring reminder that I can rest knowing my life is in His care.

THE GIFT OF A BROKEN HEART

Chapter 18

Joseph's Forgiveness

*"You intended to harm me, but God intended it for good
to accomplish what is now being done, the saving of many lives."*
- Genesis 50:20

July 11, God Makes It Good

"Father, forgive them for they know not what they do."
- Luke 23:34

Today is my husband's birthday. I prayed for him. I make myself pray for him every day to keep from becoming embittered. I cannot help my feelings, but I choose a forgiving heart toward him. Forgiving may feel like letting someone off the hook, but it is actually just freeing yourself. I will not allow anyone the power to harden my heart. Instead, I ask God to fill my heart with His grace and believe that He will use all this for good.

July 28, Release Them

*"Bear with each other and forgive one another if any of you
has a grievance against someone. Forgive as the Lord forgave you."*
- Colossians 3:13

I read in a book that one sign of emotional healing is when someone who has been abused can rejoice when others are blessed. Joseph's brothers sold him into slavery, but when they were starving and came to him for help, he did not turn them away. In fact, he generously provided for them. I want others to be blessed, but, as I pondered this, I realized that it does bother me that certain people who have badly harmed me are able to go on with their lives and be happy while I am suffering. I think this is what God wanted me to see and release. Until I can do that, my forgiveness is not complete. Again, this has more to do with freeing me than it has anything to do with those who have hurt me.

August 12, Being a Victim

"They bruised (Joseph's) feet with shackles and placed his neck in an iron collar. Until the time came to fulfill his dreams, the Lord tested Joseph's character."
- Psalm 105:18-19

God has been showing me some areas in my life that I still need to yield to Him. I want to break my bad habits, but I know that I am powerless to change these things about me. I need God. This is His work.

One of my greatest problems has to do with my expectation of being treated by others the way I treat them. When they do not, it often leads to self-pity, resentment, blame and the worst, victimhood. Yuck! I hate that. At times, I can express this through what I call *"guilt trip digs"*. Even in prison (actually, especially in here), God is giving me opportunities to see this in myself. I do not like how it looks and it is a hard thing to face. Nonetheless, I have given my life to God and that means **all** of it.

I live in a dog-eat-dog world here with many women who have had to fight their whole lives to survive. I have met many good-hearted, considerate women, but there are also plenty of bullies. A childish "me first" mentality tends to reign and expecting even the most common courtesies is a mistake. Sometimes it is tempting to respond with the same pettiness. I know the right attitude that I want to have (one of unconditional love and giving), but living it is another story.

I believe God is bringing this to my attention because He wants to heal me and teach me the meaning of grace. As I slowly become free to receive God's unconditional love, my desire to pass it on to others grows. True love has no expectation of anything in return. Nothing. Not even any thanks. This kind of transformation is a lifelong process, but it is my objective. I really do want to be able to truly love people in an unselfish, forgiving way. Yet, I know, as with everything else, my part is simply to choose it; the rest is up to God.

August 22, Haley

"But now I tell you: do not take revenge on someone who wrongs you. If anyone slaps you on the right cheek, let him slap your left cheek too."
- Matthew 5:39

One reason that I write is so that I will not miss the evidence of God's work in my life. It is so easy to forget, but when I am able to look back at my writings, I can see how everything ties together. Recently I wrote about God's transforming work in my heart to set me free to love unconditionally. It was not long before I had the opportunity to put this love into action.

My new roommate Haley has a big heart and an equally big temper. At first, we got along well and thoroughly enjoyed one another's company. Recently, however, as her release date grew closer, she became increasingly impatient and intolerant of everyone and everything. Her negative attitude and constant critical comments started getting very old, but I held my tongue until the day she put up a sign on our door listing all the people she hated. I took it down and threw it away and all hell broke loose.

Haley ranted and raged at me for a long time, threatening to tear down all my inspirational quotes and verses from the walls in retaliation. I kept my cool, apologized for taking her sign down without talking to her first, but held my ground. When she finally ran out of steam, she began a hostile silent treatment campaign that lasted for five days. She made life very uncomfortable in our little cage together and on quite a few occasions, I had to go lock myself in one of the bathroom stalls to cry out some of the hurt.

During these difficult days, I wanted "out" in the worst way, but God continued to strongly impress upon me that it was His will for me to stick this out and respond with kindness. The meaner Haley got, the more God led me to show her love. I did not attempt to talk to her much, but when I did, I kept my voice gentle, offered to share things with her and went out of my way to quietly do things for her.

Following God's leading, I was finally able to win Haley over. She apologized for how she had been treating me and opened up about her feelings. She explained to me that the unconditional love I had shown her while she was being so ugly had a huge impact on her. I was extremely relieved and so grateful to God for giving me this ability to love her and for the work He is obviously doing in her heart.

God has continued to convict Haley and give her revelations. It has been incredible to watch as she has made every effort to reconcile and make amends with others. I do not deserve credit for any of this. I am fully aware that my heart is as small and selfish as anyone else's. It was not about my good works or self discipline, as if I was gritting my teeth and working hard to behave. I am truly amazed by what God can do when you can manage to lay yourself on His altar and let Him have His way. It was not an effort to love Haley when she was hating me, because it was not <u>my</u> love. It was <u>His</u>.

September 5, Bad Rewards

"Don't be upset because of sinful people;
don't be jealous of those who do wrong..."
Psalm 37:1

It is so frustrating to continuously witness bad behavior being rewarded. Devious intentions are actually even praised at times, while those who genuinely want to do the right thing are often squashed and even demonized. I refuse to be a sour, angry person, but sometimes I feel so resentful about it. It is so difficult when it is always in my face.

It makes me miserable to feel this way, so I wrestle with it. I do not like myself like this, yet I do not know how to change how I feel. I pray about it, but it never helps for long because every time I see another troublemaker lifted up, I am right back there again. It is even harder to forgive someone who hurts you repeatedly, when no sooner have you forgiven than they do the exact same thing again, making apologies seem so empty.

Injustice makes me angry - not just in my own life, but seeing it everywhere. As I prayed about my feelings, I looked up some verses about justice, which led me to Psalm 37. Immediately convicted, I surrendered my feelings to God through tears of repentance and thanked Him for speaking so clearly to my heart.

Who am I to hold a grudge when God has forgiven me so much? That is really the bottom line, I suppose. It is not my place to condemn, because I am every bit as much the sinner as any other. My sin may be more palatable to me; but I know that in God's eyes, we are all guilty. It is His place alone to judge. And how does He do that? With so much love, compassion and grace. I am grateful to be on the receiving end of that grace, which I need as much as anyone.

September 15, High Expectations

"He suffered and endured great pain for us, but we thought his suffering was punishment from God. He was wounded and crushed because of our sins, taking our punishment, and by His wounds we are healed." .
- Isaiah 53:4-5

I keep giving my wounds to God to heal, but sometimes I feel more wounded than ever. And I keep getting wounded. I guess there is no way to love without getting wounded. Sometimes, I know I am actually doing it to myself. I have serious rejection wounds and I recognize that there are times that I feel rejected because I have come to expect it. This hurt goes so deep that I can be oversensitive about even the smallest slight.

I have high expectations of myself, but I can also have unrealistic expectations of others. Real or imagined, I have been severely wounded by a lifetime of rejection. Still, I find comfort in remembering that Jesus was rejected and wounded in this world as well. Even more important, He will never reject me. I know that love always carries the risk of being hurt, but I am not going to stop. After all, what is the point to life without love?

September 29, Better, Not Bitter

"Joseph couldn't hold himself in any longer...
he identified himself to his brothers...
Then he broke down and wept...' I am Joseph, your brother,
whom you sold into slavery in Egypt. But don't feel badly,
don't blame yourselves for selling me. God was behind it.
God sent me here ahead of you to save lives.' "
- Genesis 45:1-5

Forgiveness is a process. There are good days and bad days - two steps forward, one step back. Sometimes there is anger; sometimes there is love and compassion. I am hurt; sometimes I feel angry - understandably so - but I am not bitter. It is a constant choice I must make to forgive those who have hurt me and to let it all go. Bitter is when I give in to those feelings, feed them and allow them to take root. As long as I am choosing to forgive, then I am forgiving.

I find consolation in reading that even Joseph struggled with forgiving his brothers. When first reunited with them, he threw them in jail. Later he welcomed them and showered them with gifts. He then accused them of stealing from him before finally revealing himself to them. I understand very well this war within Joseph and it encourages me to know this man I admire so much was as human as I am.

I have had to deal with so much coming at me for so long that I barely have a chance to come up for air - to work through one attack before I am hit with another. Because of that, it might be difficult to see my progress in all the trauma. Sometimes it is difficult for me to see, so I know it must be hard for others. Certainly, I have needed to guard my heart, sometimes distancing myself, in order to protect it. That is what Joseph was doing when he at first withheld his identity from his brothers. It has taken a tremendous effort to keep my heart soft and open, to allow love and forgiveness to reign in the midst of all the heartache of my life. Yet that is what I have chosen. I pray that one day I will have the same opportunity as Joseph did for reconciliations. For now, God sees. I know that is what counts.

Chapter 19

God's Grace

"I will save the one who loves Me.
I will keep her safe because she trusts in Me.
She will call out to Me and I will answer her.
I will be with her in times of trouble.
I will save her and honor her.
I will give her a long full life."
- Psalm 91:14-15

October 12, Loving Me

"You are priceless to Me. I love you and honor you.
Do not be afraid. I am with you. I will set you free."
- Isaiah 43:1, 4, 5

In the re-entry program, I keep hearing that if I am sorry for my crime and my mistakes, then I should want to change. However, this is not the way I personally need to be thinking; I have never had a problem with self-reflection, repenting or working toward being my best self. I certainly know that I am far from perfect and, in fact, I am usually too hard on myself. The focal point of my life at this point is on valuing myself. I have experienced enough criticism, both from others and from myself. It is time for me to embrace the beauty in me.

I know many of these women here have been living self-destructive lives and really need to change their patterns in order to survive. I am in a different place. I am here for different reasons.

What is crucial for me is to believe in myself rather than try to change myself. Honestly, I have spent most of my life trying to do that, never content that I was good enough. Of course, as always, I want to grow and heal and work toward being the Avery that God created me to be, but more importantly, I want to love and appreciate her.

October 19, Humble Thyself

"Humble yourself before the Lord, and He will lift you up."
- James 4:10

This morning, as I prayed, God convicted me about humbling myself. I often feel defensive, because I have been judged and put down. I want to hold my head up high and stand up for myself. Yet, in the process, I have sometimes allowed pride, arrogance and a rebellious, disrespectful attitude toward authority to slip in. I need to go back to humbling myself and trusting God to defend me and bring about justice.

November 29, Happy Holidays

"Those who know Your name trust in You, for You,
O Lord, do not abandon those who search for You."
- Psalm 9:10

This is one of the most difficult times of the year for me. The holiday season. The best part is that these are my last incarcerated holidays. Still, it is a very painful period. Right now, I want only to run to God to pour out my pain and seek comfort. Yet I am struggling again to fully trust in God's love because I am afraid He will bop me over the head again to "teach me a lesson". I do believe that God is all I need, but I still feel alone. I do not want to feel this way. I want my heart to be faithful to God. I want even more to be able to believe that He is truly faithful to me.

Since I was 15, I have been seeking a relationship with God. I have wanted that from God far more than I have ever wanted His gifts. I have come to understand that God is very relational and yearns for a relationship with us. His creation of women was an expression of that relational, feminine side. Nonetheless, in all these years of pursuing relationship with God, I have been more inclined to perceive Him as evasive and aloof than passionately yearning for me. Then again, I recognize that it is probably my own fears that cause me to perceive a distance between God and me. It is difficult to unlearn that human view of a father figure. It is frustrating that I continue vacillating between doubting and believing. I know the truth in spite of my lapses in confidence. God is not fickle like we are. He never moves from my side. Even if the whole world turns against me, He is ever steady and true.

December 10, Just Hold On

> *"God is within her, she will not fall;*
> *God will help her at break of day."*
> - Psalm 46:5

People tell me that I am strong, but sometimes I wonder how long until my "strong" runs out. Then I remember that it is not "my" strong, but God's and His strength is endless. I learned the hard way that my own strength will run out and I know better than to depend on it.

I talked to God through my tears about this seemingly bottomless pit of pain in me. Maybe I know now that there is a bottom to it, but will it ever be all gone? This world hurts so much and I keep holding on in hopes of some fairy tale ending that probably will not happen in this life. Life is way too painful for me and I am tired of it.

I cannot imagine going out there and starting my life over, with the many obstacles I am facing alone. Alone. Bearing the labels of violent sex-offender and felon. That is strangely surreal to me - but it is definitely real. I cannot imagine right now how I will find the energy to rebuild and fight for a new life.

I asked God to restore hope to my exhausted soul. As I was praying, a song came on my little radio. The lyrics spoke so directly to my prayer. *"Just hold on."* It feels like I have been holding on for a long time. I am not sure how much longer I really can hold on. I want to give up, but God is not through with me yet. So I will hold on one more day.

January 9, A Bar of Soap

"You go before me and follow me.
You place Your hand of blessing on my head."
- Psalm 139:5

My friend Mary brought me a gift. I had been asking God this morning to show me a sign of His love for me today in some way. I opened Mary's gift to discover a bar of Dove soap, of all things. How did she know? Of course, she did not know, could not know. But God did. I was out of soap. I recognized this as God's simple, personal way of answering my prayer - showing me His love through meeting this small unspoken need. He blessed me with a bar of soap! A little thing that meant so much to me that it brought me to tears.

When I shared with Mary that this was exactly what I had been needing, she explained that God keeps putting me on her heart and compelling her to give me gifts. She could not know that this is a love language for me - but God does, so He sent Mary. I really do feel so loved today.

January 18, Joy

"My grace is all you need.
My power is strongest when you are weak."
- 2 Corinthians 12:9

I am feeling very joyful today. God has answered my prayers and renewed my hope. He has reassured me that He is in control and will give me the strength to face anything that life brings. Once again, God has done something supernatural in my heart and I am assured that I can do all things through Christ who gives me strength. His strength. Not mine.

January 26, Empathy

"People who cry a lot are not weak;
they've just had to be strong for a very long time."
- Author unknown

I woke this morning to the sound of a woman sobbing hysterically outside my door. I went to look and found one of my neighbors, Pam sitting on the floor repeating over and over, *"My daddy died!"* She was surrounded by people so I went to my room to pray for her. I felt so sad for her. I cannot fathom how difficult it must be to lose a loved one while in prison. I have seen that happen many times and the hardest to witness is the loss of a child.

I have been immersed for so long in sorrow and pain, and I am weary of it. It is especially bad here, but this world is full of sadness and it is hard on me, as I feel the pain of others deeply. I do not understand how God allows all the misery in this world - especially the innocent victims. The women here may not be innocent, but they are definitely all victims. The only thing that makes it tolerable for me is my hope of an afterlife with no tears. I do not know how anyone can get through this life without that hope.

Chapter 20

Go Out and Face Them

This is what the Lord says to you: 'Do not be afraid or discouraged because of this vast army. For the battle is not yours, but God's. You will not have to fight this battle. Take up your position; stand firm and see the deliverance the Lord will give you. Do not be afraid; do not be discouraged. Go out to face them tomorrow, and the Lord will be with you.'"
- 2 Chronicles 20:15, 17

February 7, The Battle is His

I spent awhile on my knees deeply grieving with the Lord about my life and my fears of leaving here. My heart is completely yielded to His will, and I need Him to prepare me for my release. I want to be transformed into His image. I still feel so fragile and broken. I do not feel strong enough. I have been having dreams that I am sure come from my anxieties about going out there to face everything.

God gave me the verses in 2 Chronicles 20 today. I wrote it all down and hung it at the end of my bed to read over and over. I need God to rescue me, so I cling to this promise. I will go out and face them and the Lord will be with me. I will not be alone. He will fight for me.

February 10, Defending Myself

"Do nothing out of selfish ambition or vain conceit. Rather, in humility value others above yourselves."
- Philippians 2:3

181

I am so ready to get out of here and have a life again. I can ignore the judgment of people, as long as I can once again enjoy the pleasures of good food and spend as much time as I please soaking up the beauty of nature. I am also scared, but all I can do is trust God to give me courage and protection.

God spoke powerfully to me this afternoon as I spent time with Him. I thought about my pride and anger at the way people have judged me. I realized God is calling me to accept people looking down on me, even for things that I have not actually done. If I accept my worth, then I do not need to be validated by others. This frees me to walk in humility, receiving correction from others without being defensive - even if they are wrong.

With tears pouring down my face, I once again relinquished the good opinion of others and my desire to defend myself. Of course, I recognize all I can really do about this is to give my will to God. He will have to accomplish these changes in me, but maybe I am no longer resisting and holding Him back. I hope so.

February 14, Choose Life

I have set before you life and death, blessings and curses.
Now choose life...
that you may love the Lord your God, listen to His voice,
and hold fast to Him. For the Lord is your life."
- Deuteronomy 30:19-20

These verses are not new to me, but today God used them to speak to me in a new and profound way. He convicted me of my great desire to leave this life because of all its heartache. He is calling me to willingly accept this life He has given me, willingly choose it, because all that matters is that He is my life. I chose life. I do not know how to explain it but I feel like I crossed a significant bridge today and I will never be the same.

Though I believe that God wants me to be happy and enjoy this life, I cannot live for that. Life is not always happy. However, God has purposes to accomplish in and through me. My life here is not over until His work is completed. Even if I must spend the rest of my life in pain, I can find joy in being right where He wants me to be until He calls me Home. Because I can think of no greater joy than to lay down my life for the One I love. And what could possibly be a better reason to choose life than love?

March 13, Mercies in Disguise

> *"Blessed is the one who perseveres under trial because,*
> *having stood the test, that person will receive the crown of life*
> *that the Lord has promised to those who love Him."*
> - James 1:12

I am keeping myself focused on praying, meditating, exercising, but I am battling with feelings of hopelessness about my life. Now I have absolutely no one to talk to here, but I guess that is just as well. I know I need to run to God and not to people. I just cannot seem to learn this because I am so lonely.

I got on my knees and sobbed to God for a long time before He finally spoke to me. He let me know that I could continue to cause my own suffering by being a victim. However, ***nothing*** and ***no one*** can stop His work in my life. Therefore, I do not have to worry about the impediments in my way. I can find great joy in a life of ministering and serving Him and neither my past nor anyone's opinion of me will prevent that. I can be miserable, feeling sorry for myself and worrying about all that could happen, or I can go back to enjoying the rest of this timeout and let God worry about my circumstances and my future. I cannot do a thing to fix any of it anyway. I know, I know...Duh...I have known all of this. But, now and then, He has to pull me back from the brink of hysteria and near-insanity. I am a slow learner.

I often feel like God shows me no mercy. Therefore, after an hour on my knees with God, I was listening to the Christian radio station and a song I love was playing. This line stood out to me as God's response to my complaint about His mercy.

"Maybe the trials of this life are God's mercies in disguise."

Ok. Actually, I am aware of the truth in those words. So back I go again. Waiting. Trusting. Stop running ahead in my mind to a future that does not yet exist.

March 19, Gotta Get Better

"There really is hope for you tomorrow."
- Proverbs 23:18

I spent some time praying tonight. Though I could not really pray much. I put on the radio hoping for worship music and several songs came on about holding on, it's almost over, things are going to get better. One thing is for sure: I have nowhere to go but up!

April 2, Guiding Lamp

"Your Word is a lamp to guide my feet and a light for my path."
- Psalm 119:105

As I figured, I had to register again before I leave. I came back feeling so, so depressed. I grieved for a while, and then decided to meditate and listen to some encouraging music. I have no one at all to talk to and that is hard, but I brought it to God and He got me through it, giving me some good tools to help.

I am going to do my best to be peaceful in my last days here and focus on God's love. I have not been as faithful in recent months about speaking scripture to encourage myself, so I hung up my papers with verses to resume reading them every day. I always find that uplifting.

God's Word has become essential to my survival and I continue to be in awe of how relevant it is to my own life. The stories of suffering and overcoming in the Bible of people like Job, David, and Joseph have come to life for me as they have guided me through the deep waters. I have felt their pain and been inspired by their courage. They have been like friends, cheering me on and making the way seem less lonely. This ancient book is more than just an outdated relic, but rather a life raft that has been carrying me through many storms.

April 16, Starting Over

"With God, all things are possible."
- Matthew 19:26

I feel better today. I am trying to focus on the positive, so I am starting to feel positive again. I am starting to become excited and curious to see what God has for me out there. I know I have so much potential and I am not going to let anyone's judgment stand in my way. I feel like my life is just beginning and I have got lots of lost time to make up for and lots of great stuff to do. One thing I want to remember is to do something that scares me every day.

Look out world! Here I come! The REAL AVERY is about to start living. And she's a powerful force! Well, to be more accurate - she's got a powerful force behind her!

April 20, Build Me Up

"I have loved you with a love that lasts forever.
I have kept on loving you with faithful love.
I will build you up again.
You will go out and dance with joy."
- Jeremiah 31:3-4

Time is dragging, dragging, though I am at peace and content enough. I am feeling tired and unmotivated, but trying to be gentle with myself and enjoy my last few days of "vacation" from life with no responsibilities. At the same time, I am so excited about the many things I can experience again that I have been missing.

This morning, I broke down and poured out some more pain to God about my kids. I pray He will give me the ability to love them unconditionally, in spite of my heartache. I know that God has been building me up in preparation for my release and strengthening my faith. I no longer have any fear or anxiety, just a confidence that God is going to bless me and do great things in my life.

April 24, Out of the Gate

"I know the plans I have for you, says the Lord.
Plans to prosper you and not to harm you.
Plans to give you hope and a future."
- Jeremiah 29:11

This will be my last entry as a prison inmate! How fitting that I am being released on Good Friday. It is a good Friday indeed! I am most grateful for My Savior's sacrifice of His life for mine. No matter what happens, I am in God's mighty hands.

I had a marvelous prayer time on my knees before the Lord, filled with gratitude for all He has done in my life these past few years. My whole heart and life are committed to God and His will. I have never felt such confidence and peace in His care for me. I am excited to see what great things He has in store. He really has done so much healing and transforming in my heart. I am feeling His love intensely like a strong tower around me. I am ready to go out and face them. So...

"Forgetting the past and looking forward to what lies ahead, I press on..."
- Phil 3:13

THE BEGINNING.

Acknowledgements

Thank you to my Lord for His Holy Word which has been my greatest source of inspiration, truth and wisdom. I would also like to thank my dear friend Fozzie for being my unofficial, but most diligent editor and biggest cheerleader. Thanks to all who have loved and supported me throughout this effort. Thanks also to each of you who have taken the time to read my first book and to all who have been led to share it with others.

As you have surely noticed, my story is not over and there is still much more to tell. If you are interested in learning more about my journey, stay tuned. I shall return.

ABOUT THE AUTHOR

Avery Garrett Long has been a artist, teacher, nurse, manager, secretary, caregiver, taxi driver, and counselor - all at the same time. Now that she is a famous author, she spends her time relaxing on a tropical beach with a fruity drink and a good book. She is passionate about empowering other women and dancing in the rain - naked, if possible. The wisest advice she ever got came from her mother, who often told her, *"Life's not fair. Get over it"*, which Avery has found to be true and most helpful to remember.

Made in the USA
Coppell, TX
17 May 2020

25858211R00113